L E T T E R S

FROM THE

Y E A R S

LETTERS FROM THE *Middle* YEARS

Martha Morgan Kern

LION
PUBLISHING

Lion Publishing
A division of Cook Communications,
4050 Lee Vance View
Colorado Springs, Colorado 80918

Editor: Greg Clouse
Design: Bill Gray
Interior Design: Cheryl Ogletree

1 2 3 4 5 6 7 8 9 10 Printing/Year 02 01 00 99 98

Table of Contents

For my father,
who always believed I could do it.

Acknowledgments

All books, even those as personal as this one, represent a collaborative effort. Every person I have known on my journey has somehow influenced me, and thus somehow influenced this work. Though I obviously cannot thank everyone individually, I would like to single out a few who have been particularly helpful in the creation of this volume: Douglas Balz, managing editor of the *Chicago Tribune Magazine*, who was the first to publish my work; Greg Clouse, my editor at Lion Publishing, whose vision and guidance made this book a reality; and, especially, my many friends and family members who patiently tolerate both the joys and agonies of being included in my stories. While my gratitude to them is immense and quite public, their names have been changed herein to protect their privacy.

Chapter 1

Dear Gary

"It finally occurred to me
that my deepest and
most persuasive fear centered
around 'coming out'
as a believer in God,
which this book will ultimately
nudge me into doing."

Dear Gary,

I t occurs to me as I prepare to write this book of ours, this collection of letters, that I should tell you a little about myself and my work and the feelings that float around these things like buoys at sea. We are mere acquaintances, you and I, having come together through a series of random or providential events, to make a book appear where none appeared before. As a publisher, you have given me a unique privilege, really, to talk to a larger audience, or a different one, and you have given it to me for no reason other than that you believe I can do it, and do it well. I wish I were as confident. I wish I could be sure.

Certainty is, quite possibly, one of life's more elusive prizes. I have never had it for longer than a minute or two and even then its outlines were a bit ghostly. I would love to be more certain of my place in the world, my purpose in this life, my ability to leave behind some sign that I lived here that will last on and on, like initials carved deep in a tree. But my self-doubt will stay as long as it is comfortably entwined in the arms of its keeper, the one who tells stories in the night's deep darkness, the one who gently insists that confidence is the province of other people and suits me no better than a flaming red cape or a lesson in boxing. It will stay as long as Fear is there to hold it.

There can be no doubt that we all have fear to one degree or another. Perhaps you are afraid of heights or hypodermic needles. I know people who are afraid to fly, afraid to speak up or show their feelings or walk the streets after 9 p.m. While I don't mind flying and have recently learned to face down the spiders that tiptoe along my ceilings, I might on any given day awaken to find myself afraid of death, afraid of changing, afraid of staying the same, afraid of being afraid in perpetuity (though strangely unafraid to say so). And now, Gary, as I begin the writing of this book, I carry in my hands an unwelcome but seductively familiar fear of failure.

I imagine that fear of failure has caused many a book to go unwritten, many hobbies to remain untried, many careers to be quietly though thoroughly spoiled. Fear always chooses safety over risks, the status quo over something new. Had you let you fear get the better of you, Gary, you might not have packed up your family and their many accessories to take a new position in Colorado. But whatever fear you might have felt, you somehow pushed aside. Maybe it took awhile. Maybe you considered staying here, taking a less challenging position, looking for something local so as not to uproot the kids. You might have told yourself during the bleakest moments of some sleepless night that a larger corporation was not for you. You might have assured yourself that no community, no church, could ever be as personally fulfilling as the ones you already had. You might have convinced yourself that answering the call of a new opportunity would cause you to somehow trip over its velvety carpets and fall into a humbled, defeated heap.

I feel a little funny saying that to you, Gary, because I don't know you that well. But I don't really need to know all about you or anyone else to know that each of us harbors a little bit of fear in our hearts like children cradle anxieties in their night-darkened rooms. I think fear is one of the things that makes us all alike, yet keeps us oddly separate from one another. We let it stand between us, cold river that it is, and stop us from taking the sort of chances with one another that make vulnerability an everyday thing and love a real possibility. Afraid to be intimate with one another, we become intimate with fear instead.

I haven't told you this yet, but I came very close to scaring myself away from writing this book. Almost as soon as I felt joy and exhilaration at the prospect of writing it, I began to talk myself down. I told myself it wouldn't work. As a Christian book publisher, you might, to my thinking, ask me to write things that were stylistically and thematically off my map. A few people reminded me that, at this relatively early point in my career, I could be limited, even damaged, by a spiritual public identity. So with the help of those around me, I set up barricades in the road to avoid the painful fact that fear was at the wheel. The plan taking shape in my subconscious mind was to avoid the possibility of failure altogether by taking no chance at all.

What I was also avoiding were the deeper concerns that lay

just beneath this smoke screen of professional issues. I did not care to contemplate that, despite a steady if not glorious track record, I may not be able to come up with the goods. There might be a sudden drought in my thinking, a creative abyss where no ideas would come forth, or no words would properly honor those that did. I imagine all writers have this oily specter nibbling at the edge of their psyches. It has become a companion of mine, and for reasons I can't fully grasp, I am not yet ready to give it up.

And, more important, I have been, to some degree, unwilling to give up the spiritual limbo in which I have lived for many years. It finally occurred to me that my deepest and most persuasive fear centered around "coming out" as a believer in God, which this book will ultimately nudge me into doing. Taking a stance has never been my strong suit. Publicly declaring myself to be a specific person of a particular mind, supporter of this and detractor of that, is not my modus operandi. I like to keep my options open. I am one who agonizes over small decisions and considers too many viewpoints in trying to formulate my own; it is hard for me to take one position when it requires that I pass up all the other thoughtful ideas that lay before me like appetizers on a tray. I am wishy-washy about many issues of our day. And I have been wishy-washy, even a little lazy, about committing myself to God.

Suddenly I see that I am as flimsy and fickle as a teenaged girl and it is this realization that has finally inspired me to risk being known as a specific person of a particular mind.

Consider this letter, Gary, and those that will accompany it, as that risk embodied. In the writing of this book I will be exploring many of my oldest and most cherished neuroses, my strengths and my weaknesses, the tenor of my relationships, both human and divine. In it my soul will be exhibited like a piece of modern art, and I will be accountable for its condition. It will be the best that I can do today.

Am I certain that I will fulfill the task before me? Not completely, but I will commit myself to it anyway. I don't really feel that I have a choice. I must face the prospect of failure or risk falling asleep to the sound of my life ticking by. In spite of all my rationalizations and hesitations and intellectual arguments to the contrary, it seems that I was put here to take chances and maybe even to occasionally fail in the process. My fear-slackened muscles are screaming for a chance to run. It is time to get moving. It is time to take a stand. It is time to become the person God made me to be, the spiritual adventurer, the doer, the worker, the writer who writes.

Are you ready, Gary? Well then, let's get going.

With hope and resolve,

M

Chapter 2

Dear Dan,

"I want the faith and hope that
you offer, but in the deep
recesses of my mind I feel
they will somehow unravel me,
that all I can really afford is
a small taste of those
tantalizing pleasures."

Dear Dan,

In writing a letter to you, I am hoping to make contact in a way that is impossible on Sunday; the busy passages of church, full of people who are looking specifically for you, are not a place for meaningful dialogue. As pastor, you are a source of divine fuel for those of us whose lanterns burn low by the end of the week. There is an energy about you, a knowingness, that most of us hope to catch like some pleasant strain of flu. You've got something that all of us want for ourselves.

Surely, you know it. You are aware of your gifts for leadership, communication, and spiritual insight. You have the unique ability to make people feel as if they have been selected for some special purpose. When I listen to you speak, your charisma runs over me like warm, fragrant water, and it scares me to death. I resist it in the way that a dieter of weak resolve resists sizzling sausages or fat, gooey pastries; I want the faith and hope that you offer, but in the deep recesses of my mind I feel they will somehow unravel me, that all I can really afford is a small taste of those tantalizing pleasures.

I imagine this sounds a little strange to you, Dan. I should remind you that yours is the first church I have attended in twenty years—I come now not as a sullen, resentful teenager, but as a questioning, cautious adult. I am a seeker who reaches out hungrily one day and retreats the next. You call, God calls, and I lift my feet to walk, only to find they are weighted with concerns and trepidation, an independent woman's leeriness of governance and structure and a way of life that is free, perhaps, in the superficial way young children's are; they can do what they like only as far as the parental reins extend.

My independence is something I protect and cherish as a violinist shields her instrument. It is something I had to create for myself, really work for, after years and years of habitual dependence. In my parents' house, movements toward free thought and self-reliance were quickly circumvented; my father, especially, believed his control over me would keep me safe, like a seat belt or a thick coating of Teflon, in a world where influences were dark and disasters forever imminent. He made decisions for me; my father led, I followed. It was a system that worked, in its own way. And then, sudden as a kitchen fire, he died.

At the age of twenty, I became fatherless and lost. Without the guiding structure of a college schedule, I might easily have wandered from the track of my life and laid myself down in the grass. It was difficult, a form of torture, to make decisions for myself. But learning to stand on my own became my most important course of study, and it is an effort toward which I expended considerable time and focus. Having leaned too heavily on a pillar that would eventually crumble, I was determined to never be let down again. I would rely on no one but myself. All I really needed, I thought, was me.

Well, as you might expect, I became quite independent. Over these many years I have used my independence like a gate, keeping out the people who might try to influence me or advise me or make me weak with their support and assistance, and keeping myself walled in, safe from the perils of disappointment and unexpected reversal. Certainly, I have loved and been loved, hurt and been hurt, but I have never fully depended on other people; as a free agent, I can dismiss the trespasses of others with an indifferent shrug. Who needs them, anyway? All in all, it is a predictable place, this world of mine, and it is empty as a bottomless cavern.

Perhaps it was this emptiness, Dan, that first brought me to your door. I was tired and in need of some comfort. Church seemed like an excellent place in which to find the meaning and joy that were lacking in my life, to build my strength for the rest of the trip. But where I was hoping to feel more independent and sure-footed and super-sufficient, I find I am sensing my own neediness more by the day. God's Word has shown me his power, and beside it I stand as a flimsy, anemic reed. It has finally dawned on me, Dan, that God is inherently antithetical to aloneness, unimpressed by independence, and not at all inclined to being a benevolent outsider, a mere witness to a life that I am running on my own. God, it seems, wants to help. He wants to support and enlighten and point the way. He wants me to let him in. I want to, Dan, but the latch on my gate has become rusty with disuse; it will take some work, some patience, to open it.

There is a part of me that believes help, divine or otherwise, delivered consistently and effectively and lovingly, will cause me to fall permanently, painfully, to my knees. If I become reliant on you or my friends or my family or God, most of all, will I lose my balance, my determination, my ability to stand up straight? Will I be that child again, the one who borrowed opinions, shied away from decisions, and hesitated, perplexed and uncertain, at each fork in the road? If the gate swings open, will my independence billow up and vanish like chimney smoke in the cold night air? When I tally up the potential losses, it seems a terrible bet.

This is where you come in, Dan. I look at you and listen to your words and I see a person of accomplishment, of strength, of buoyancy and courage; you have staked it all on God, committed your whole life to serving him and, still, there is no sign of weakness or loss. I see not a person defeated and made useless by his reliance on God, but one who is moved by it, encouraged, encircled by a limitless ocean of acceptance and assurance. It seems to me that God is the only gate you need and within it, he stands beside you. You are independent, forever entitled to the free will God gave you, yet you are never alone.

Perhaps it is not my independence that will flee when my gate is finally pried open.

It may be my aloneness or the distance I have placed between me and those I love. My need for control might escape, along with the ungainly burden of walking life's route by myself.

And into my gate might flow companionship, community, mutual reliance, and unabashed affection. I may, by letting God in, sacrifice only the puffed-up pride of one who has stood, stubbornly and foolishly, on her own two aching feet when God was willing to cushion the ground and even to occasionally carry her, simply for the asking.

It appears I have some repairs to make in my life, some old barriers to dismantle. And Dan, though it pains me a bit to say it, I could really use your help.

With hope and determination,

M

Chapter 3

Dear Uncle Joe,

"I wished at that moment
that I had long ago traded in
my messy tangle of layered
defenses and tortuous rationales
for the cleansing, weightless
privilege of confessing
a wrong and making it right."

Dear Uncle Joe,

Years have passed since I've written you a letter and, I can assure you, I have never written to you in the style that I will today. Let's set aside the newsy material for another time, shall we? (Everyone here is fine. The weather remains unpredictable.) What I would like to discuss with you today is a subject which has recently been tagging after me like a child with nothing better to do; perhaps it has to do with my age or maturity or emergent spiritual consciousness, but lately I have been thinking about cheating and its effect on the soul.

When I refer to cheating here, I am not talking about marital infidelities or the sort of wholesale fraud that occurs among government officials and white-collar embezzlers. I am talking instead about the smaller forms of cheating we all engage in, the little swindles and petty larcenies that smudge our daily lives like tiny flecks of ink. You know what I mean: the passing of pale, white lies; exceeding the speed limit simply because we can; keeping the extra quarter the cashier inadvertently offers; using the phone at the office to call an old friend in Canada. Few of us could say we are innocent of all such crimes; perhaps fewer of us acknowledge them, even to ourselves. The fact that they are easily overlooked, easily kept secret, reassures us in the same way that a person of large proportion is reassured by vertical stripes. As long as our outward images are pleasant enough, we can occasionally indulge in a light deceit and perhaps even succeed in tricking ourselves; a clever, undetected lie becomes even more real, more engaging, than the truth itself.

Perhaps by now, Uncle Joe, you have grasped the reason this letter is addressed to you. You are probably remembering, as I am, that unsavory incident in Southern California, circa 1981. You and I have never really talked about that episode; it has been my desire to forget it, and yours, I imagine, to minimize my humiliation. While I appreciate your attempts to preserve my dignity, I would now like to examine some of my shadier impulses and try to understand them, just as a cat might try to fathom her instinct to scratch.

I was about twenty-four when we came to visit you in California, and I remember it as a fine though slightly frantic trip. We packed in a lot of activity, including a morning of junk-hunting at a number of different garage sales. It was at one such sale that I found a beautiful spice cabinet; it was wooden and heavy, a substantial piece of craftsmanship, and alongside its shelves for spices were glassed-in rows of beans, rice, and other dried, colorful foods. The cabinet spoke to me on some irrational level and, despite a price that exceeded my budget, I decided to buy it.

As a visitor in the days before cash machines were rampant, I offered the owner a traveler's check in lieu of cash. He graciously accepted it, and then graciously proceeded to give me $10 in excess change. I wish I could tell you that I didn't notice the overage while there was still time to correct it, but I did notice it and I did not correct it. I walked away from the smiling man with a lovely spice cabinet and an illicit satisfaction over my unexpected cash rebate.

Do you remember my sharing this bit of news with you? I told you, as soon as we reached the car, and I recall sensing immediately that you were disappointed in me. You didn't say anything, Uncle Joe, but your expression was one of moral confusion; you wanted to give me the approval I was looking for, but couldn't bring yourself to do it. I related the story to you in hopes of gaining an ally, in hopes of banishing my guilt, but instead was faced with the queasy truth that I had done something wrong. I knew it, and worse, you knew it too.

Still, I did not remedy the problem while I had the chance, there at the sale. I didn't want to give up what I'd gathered, even if it was an inconsequential sum, even if it was an ill-gotten prize. My mind must have provided me with a litany of face-saving excuses: these people obviously had more money than me, perhaps the man meant to give me a discount, the spice cabinet was not worth their asking price in the first place. Having reassured myself of my own essential rightness, at least to the degree that I could go on posing as an honest citizen, I released the matter from my consciousness like a school teacher dismisses her class. I resolved to be finished with it because it was too painful, too complex, to consider my own character as something wrinkled, uneven, defective.

Although I would have liked to continue my vacation in rationalized bliss, God had other ideas. By no other hand than his did that garage-sale man turn up in the same fish-market parking lot as we did the very next day. The man remembered me. He approached me nicely, explaining that he had unwittingly undercharged me and wanted to collect his money. I stood there, thoroughly off-guard, and made the subconscious choice to cheat a little more. Instead of seizing the opportunity God gave me to repent and make things right, I dug my trench a bit deeper and told the man I didn't know what he was talking about.

Why? I ask myself now. Was the money that important to me? I don't think it was. What mattered to me at that raw moment was something far more visceral: I wanted to keep what had become mine, I wanted to hug it to my chest like a puny life preserver, I wanted to hold on to this insignificant thing because to let go of it would require that I also let go of my good-girl image, my self-wrought delusion that whatever I did was okay as long as it could be resculpted, explained away, made to look legitimate. It would require that I confess to the world that I was weak, flawed, wrong, after years of pretending not to be. So I held on to the money and held on to a self-image that could wear no thinner and sink no lower. I gained $10, but I lost my soul.

It wasn't until many years later that I was told you repaid the man after I'd gone back home to Chicago. My shame at this revelation was great, and it was deserved. But instead of discounting your action as something absurdly moral or prudish, I recognized it as simple, right-hearted, an act without burden or remorse. I wished that I had done it myself. I wished at that moment that I had long ago traded in my messy tangle of layered defenses and tortuous rationales for the cleansing, weightless privilege of confessing a wrong and making it right. At some point in those intervening years I had evidently learned a thing or two about the cumbersome nature of deceit and the relief that flows from seeing the truth and saying its name out loud.

It might hearten you to know that the Lord continued to offer me lessons through that notorious spice cabinet. Despite our careful packaging for the trip home, the cabinet window was violated by a diagonal crack, a permanent bolt of lightening, by the time it arrived at my house. Even more fitting is the odd justice contained in the cabinet's dark interior: it was infested with minute, determined bugs who, over the course of a year or two, nibbled away at the glassed-in beans and noodles until they were nothing but dust.

Like me, the cabinet had maintained a facade of structural integrity, but was deeply compromised within. Only God could speak so eloquently.

With gratitude,

M

P.S. The Lord recently gave me yet another opportunity to repay that old debt. I was erroneously given a check for $15 (God apparently added $5 to the original amount to allow for inflation) and, this time, I promptly gave it back.

Chapter 4

Dear Dad,

"The ceaseless management of
details can sometimes
supplant the dreaming of dreams,
the remembering of memories,
the contemplation of the
true purpose, the true meaning,
of the lives that we've
been given."

Dear Dad,

I t's been a long time since we've talked, almost twenty years, almost half my life; your spirit left this earth when I was twenty years old, and now I'm nearing forty. I wonder sometimes if you would still recognize me. I wonder too if you would be pleased with the woman I've become. I am, in many ways, very much like the child I used to be, the one who worked alongside you every Saturday morning, advancing from errand to errand, the car stopping just long enough for me to hop out and run to the dry cleaners, the hardware store, the watch repair shop, while you circled the block and contemplated the next leg of our purposeful mission. We were efficient, in perfect synchrony, chiming together gloriously like church bells in a tower.

You see, Dad, I've always thought of you as the man who showed me the value and meaning of hard, honest work.

There would be no me if there had been no you; it was you who taught me to have self-discipline, a willingness to work diligently, a reverent regard for responsibility. You believed in the sanctity of one's jobs, one's duties in this life, and in the importance of meeting obligations. Your belief in these things was dynamic and contagious, certain and emphatic, and it was a salve for my unfocused soul. You were my mentor, and I your protégé. You were the boom and I was your echo.

Though it rarely registered in my consciousness, I had two very distinct and irreconcilable models from which to choose in fashioning my own persona. There was Mom, of course, who pursued her passions and left life's less glamorous obligations among the cobwebs in the china cabinet. She liked to listen to the radio well into the night, and then to sleep deeply as the commotion of morning swirled all around her. It was her habit to let dust and dirty laundry accumulate, to leave beds unmade until 4 p.m. and dinners unplanned until 5, to watch television and talk on the phone when your shirts, laundered but too wrinkled to wear, lay in a forgotten heap on the ironing board. The more you hounded her to care for the house, to do her job, the more she rebelled. Mom's idea of joy and fulfillment lay somewhere outside the sphere of chores and domestic particulars, and somewhere well outside the realm of our more task-driven sensibilities.

And then there was you, Dad, who seemed to work every second of every day, hustling off to the office in the morning and then back home at night, studying the events of the world, writing letters to the editor of every paper in town, staining the woodwork on weekends, painting fences, lugging firewood, raking mountains of leaves from the yard. I remember it was my job to sit on the bottom of your extension ladder as you washed the second-floor windows. I remember the lessons you gave me in the meticulous cleaning of bathrooms (don't forget to polish the fixtures) and the afternoons we spent wiping fingerprints from all the switch plates in the house with rags soaked in Fantastik. You were teaching me to care about details others would overlook. You were teaching me to work until the last chore was done, tirelessly and with great intention, to labor for the simple joy of doing a job and doing it well.

I suppose it should give me great satisfaction to report to you that those lessons were thoroughly learned, and they are imprinted within me like a genetic code. My house runs on a schedule as reliable as a train's. I do the laundry every three or four days; each dresser in the house is stuffed with clean clothing, all lightly scented with fabric softener. The rooms are dusted and vacuumed, and scuff marks are removed from the kitchen floor almost as soon as they appear in their streaky, black formations. I tend to the children's needs, I work on my writing every morning, I keep track of library books and dental appointments, drive the kids to this class and that, and sit down only for dinner. My litany of chores determines my mood for the day, and whether or not there will be time left for something as plain, as lazy, as reading a book to my son.

It is all very starched and organized, this life of mine, but, like yours, it lists to one side, supremely out of balance, heavy on anxiousness and rather light on fun, a study in motion and discipline and the steady drip-drip of energy leaking from the soul. It is not the work itself I regret, but the compulsion, the devotion to busyness, that underlies it. The ceaseless management of details can sometimes supplant the dreaming of dreams, the remembering of memories, the contemplation of the true purpose, the true meaning, of the lives that we've been given.

When you think of it, Dad, obsessively seeing to life's minor obligations allows us to sidestep its larger panorama and the difficult scenes within it. It is easier to worry about stains in the carpet than it is about smudges on our characters. It is less taxing to run from errand to errand than to sit still and reflect on the paths we are afraid to wander.

Maybe because I am just ten years shy of the age at which your short life came to its sudden conclusion, I find myself reassessing. Perhaps because I've begun to understand that even my greatest efforts and most strenuous concentration will not render this life fully manageable nor bring it within my control, I have conceded my need for help and rest and a renewed sense of direction. I believe God had more in mind for me than I have taken the time to imagine or found the courage to explore.

When I think of you now, Dad, I envision what it would be like to have you show up at my house on a Saturday morning, unexpected but not in your usual hurry, carrying an envelope of news clippings you've saved for me and a bag of fresh cherries from the farm stand you frequent. You and my husband would talk quietly in the kitchen, we'd have coffee, the kids would surround you with the soft flannel of their pajamas, and we would be a family in that blessed, ordinary moment.

You see, Dad, when I allow myself to just sit and dream, I dream of what we might have been to each other if only we'd had the time.

With love,

M

Chapter 5

Dear Cab Driver,

"Despite our obvious
differences, it apparently
occurred to you that I might
know exactly how you felt
as you looked for some way to
seize back your dignity
from a man who had no business
taking it."

Dear Cab Driver,

Before we get down to the nitty-gritty of this letter, let me assure you that it's perfectly understandable if you don't remember me or our ride together many years ago. It would be something of a miracle if you did. I'm sure that, for you, the ride was as unremarkable as the highway guard rails that seem to run along beside you all day like mindless dogs. It was nothing, you might say, just a trip to the airport.

You picked me up, I believe, at the John Hancock Center in Chicago, the building in which I worked back in the mid-1980s. In my late twenties at the time, I was blonder than I am now, petite, probably looking a lot more cool and purposeful than I felt. I was likely wearing a dress of some kind, carrying a briefcase and one of those hang-up suitcases full of zippered compartments and clever contrivances. In those days, I traveled a lot and rode in plenty of cabs; except for those few that were crisscrossed inside by a thousand hanging pompoms, thick with the scent of coconut, or driven by buzzardy old men who talk-talk-talked in maddening circles, yours is the only one I remember.

Looking back on you, my memory summons up a small, wiry man, someone who, though not muscular, could likely take care of himself if called upon to do so. I recall a chestnut-colored face, spongy dark hair, a hooded sweatshirt, a pair of jeans. I remember too that you had an easy way about you, an accessibility that stood in contrast to my more cautious posture. We were a study in opposites, you could say; anyone who saw us would think us an odd couple, I suppose, a pineapple and a tomato temporarily residing in the same wicker basket.

It's difficult to recall how the subject of crime first sidled into our conversation. You were telling me a story about some guy, a troublemaker, who lived in the same housing project as you. He had done something, said something—I don't remember what—that enraged you and your friends thoroughly, deep in your bones, all the way down to that black-blackest point where nothing much matters but the fury's rough texture. The guy messed with you. He offended you or insulted you or made you look foolish. As you spun the story there in the cab, you looked at me in the rearview mirror, shrugged your shoulders, and said, "There was only one thing to do. We had to go back and get the steel." By that, you explained, you meant guns, knives, chains, the weapons of the street. I don't know if it was your intention to kill that man or not, but it was clearly your plan to go out and find him again, to wave a gun in his face and see if it didn't change his perspective somewhat.

I returned your look in the rearview mirror and nodded my head. I nodded in assent, in understanding, as if to say, "Well, of course that's what you did," or, "What else could you do?" Maybe I even created the unreasonable impression that this was the way things were done in my world too, that the fetching of guns and the stalking of neighbors was an ordinary, so-what kind of thing that everybody does. At that moment, I stepped out of my own white-girl, nothing's-up community and willing-ly, gladly, walked a step or two into yours. I wanted to see what lay behind this strange, inviting door that you held open.

Thinking back on this, Cab Driver, I wonder what it was about me that led you to tell this story in the first place. Dressed for business as I was, not at all the tough-ish type that knows the streets, I sat in the backseat positively radiating middle-class blandness, I'm sure. But you chose this story, this tale of urban revenge and criminal intent, to unspool before me like an epic movie as we cruised toward the airport.

Perhaps you thought you might shock me or make me squirm a bit there in your cab. Even though I was the one who got to name our destination and I was the one who was techni-cally in charge, it was your cab, your turf, your story to tell. Once you made it known that you were armed at least some of the time, the balance of power shifted from the backseat to the front; it was understood by both of us that you were captain of this particular ship.

But I think there was something else afoot, something even more subtly influential than your ego or my desire for a vicari-ous adventure. As a cab driver, you might read people and situ-ations as easily as the rest of us read headlines. You might be able to sense that even those who have never brandished a gun to even out a lopsided playing field have at least wished, for just one split second in their otherwise orderly, rational lives, that they could. Despite our obvious differences, it apparently occurred to you that I might know exactly how you felt as you looked for some way to seize back your dignity from a man who had no business taking it.

Several years ago, I was driving my own car on a Saturday afternoon on Chicago's north side. A traffic light abruptly changed to red, and I came to a stop with the nose of my Honda Civic extending a small distance into the crosswalk. As I waited for the light to change yet again, two men crossed the street in front of me. Very suddenly, one of them charged over to my car and started screaming about the fact that the crosswalk had been slightly breached by my bumper. And then, in spite of the fact that he was a grown man, in spite of the dozens of people who stood by watching, in spite of the alarm that must have been surging over my face like a bad case of hives, he produced an unwrapped bar of soap from his pocket and liberally smeared it over the driver's side of my windshield.

As you might imagine, Cab Driver, I was shocked at first, and then wildly angry. Not only was this man picking on a lone female for the pettiest of reasons, but he was walking around with a bar of soap in his pocket looking for an excuse to use it. He would not have done it to you, nor to any other man, nor even to a sizable woman, I'm sure. He chose me because I posed no threat. In his estimation, I was nothing more than an easy, available mark.

Even now, ten or twelve years later, I feel a tingle of adrenalin when I think of it. I have replayed that scene in my mind many times, with a host of outcomes more satisfying than dull reality provided. I picture myself running after the guy and pushing him down on the sidewalk. I've wondered what it would have been like to chase him down and pin him to a wall with my car. And, at my very worst, I've imagined the horrified look his face might take on if I pointed a gun out my window and made him clean away the soap with his shirt.

You are probably snickering to yourself over this, Cab Driver; even you, a virtual stranger, can quickly discern that I am not the type of person who would ever actually do any of those things. I hate guns and have never owned one. I've never intentionally threatened or injured anyone—I don't even spank my kids. But deep inside the lining of my heart, I've experienced the same anguished helplessness, the same rapid-hot flowering of pain and rage, the same dark impulses that shuddered through your system on that sweltering night in the projects. I nodded my head as you told your story not because I agreed with your violent methods, but because I understood the subterranean feelings that drove them. At that moment, you and I connected in a way I would otherwise have thought impossible.

Like everyone else, I suppose, you and I share a familiarity with raggedy, unmanageable desires, a stubborn, unforgiving burn in our chests when another person shows us contempt or disrespect. A theft occurs, really. Our spirits are momentarily plundered. We feel, sometimes, as if we are alone, alien, under siege from those around us. It is a cold, cruel world and in it, we work to survive. But now and then, we get an unexpected gift, as I did that day in your cab. I was reminded not of our obvious differences, our apart-ness and diversity, but of our subtle sameness and our universal bondedness. We are spiritually the same, equal, no one better than the other, individual char-acters in the same divine drama, struggling with the same con-voluted plots and impenetrable subtexts. It is a simple truth, but I tend to forget it.

You and me and the soap man and your troublemaker, we are all passengers on the same wild ride. Sometimes, the ride is especially good and we feel the warm presence of the travelers on either side of us, and we remember, however fleetingly, that we are never quite alone and our problems are not all that singular. If we're very lucky, we occasionally feel understood and possibly even forgiven for being what we are. Thinking of us all as such, I feel my ancient wounds and irritations, my me-against-you isolation, melting away like soap on a hot windshield. It is eas-ier to let go of transgressions if it is a twin of my own flawed and needy spirit I am forgiving.

Thanks for the ride, Mr. Cab Driver. It was a doozy.

M

Chapter 6

Dear Mark,

"I was just gliding along until
your death stopped me,
and I paused long enough to ask
'What am I doing?'
and I looked at my spirit,
hanging limp at the back
of my closet."

Dear Mark,

The thought of you, old friend, evokes a mishmash of feeling in me. On the one hand, I want to laugh; you were always so funny, clever beyond all reason, a moving field of energy, and I find myself smiling as I remember. There were long summer evenings full of wry adventure, and countless episodes of story-making proportion. Boredom was forfeited when you were around, Mark, and sadness was shelved, out of sight, like rows of jarred preserves in a farmhouse cellar.

But then, on the other hand, your name conjures up an unbearable blend of grief and confusion. I cannot think of your life, Mark, without also thinking of your death. It was horrible, coming as it did, completely unforeseen and so early in your journey. One day you were here, bounding around, working hard, married to my dear cousin and raising four small kids, and the next day you weren't. You went on a routine business trip to the West Coast and, for no reason anyone could fathom, died in your hotel room. Just like that, a heart attack came and left with you.

At first I was buoyed by a thick layer of unbelief. How could this be? You were only thirty-five and as healthy as the rest of us. It just didn't seem possible, and my rational mind would have no part of it. But finally, Mark, I saw you, and I knew that it was true. The spirit that once lived within your body and made it such a welcome presence had moved on to a place beyond our earthbound senses, outside our human grasp.

You probably saw the havoc your departure created; to say that there was grieving and shock, anger and heartache, would not begin to say it all. When someone dies so abruptly and so young, we are not afforded the comfort of a life full-lived—we cannot reassure ourselves that it's for the best, or take refuge in the predictable, accepted scheme of youth fading gradually into old age, and then gradually into peaceful death. Instead, we are rudely confronted with mortality's deep mysteries, its refusal to be pinned down or read like sodden tea leaves, its ability to surprise and ruin us, again and again. We are forcefully reintroduced to the cruel truth that death is not fair, it is not preventable, and it will come for us too. When I came face-to-face with your mortality, Mark, I came face-to-face with my own as well.

Certainly, I had pondered my own demise before your passing. During my second pregnancy, when I was found to have precancerous cells flourishing on my cervix, I entertained the specter of cancer and the stark possibility that my children might grow up motherless. That same summer, as I awaited results on this biopsy or that, an old friend of mine died of cancer; he was thirty-five and the father of two. It rocked me, Mark, and death's blurry image began to come into kaleidoscope focus. I wasn't ready to see it, though, and I shaded my eyes, terrified, fascinated, ambivalent as a gaper creeping past an auto wreck.

But when you died a few years later, Mark, there would be no such reprieve. After a short period of steadfast avoidance, I could look away no more. Unwilling and unwitting, I fell headlong into a chilly season of spiritual crisis.

Suddenly, the clock was ticking. Death made me more aware of life and its inescapable brevity. Everything I had once taken for granted came under my intense scrutiny; urgently, I reassessed virtually every facet of my life, and I wasn't happy with what I found. Not only had I abandoned many of my dreams, but I had become a slave to my paycheck, a junkie whose drug was the approval of others, a soul whose core was essentially empty. Mark, I was going through the motions of middle life, caught up in the beat of the workaday world, keeping my children dressed and fed, running my house, when it finally occurred to me that all this dancing is meaningless if there is no music. If life's many machinations have no underlying purpose, I reasoned, then they serve merely as an absurd and stressful prelude to death.

For me, facing the reality of death, Mark, meant facing the reality of life, its numerous tangents and beckoning avenues, its somber ramifications and superficial pursuits, its unavoidable pointlessness without the possibility of eternity, the promise of God. You could say that death's imposing deadline brought me back to life.

I had always been a believer in God, but my belief was soft, flimsy, unimpressive in its texture and scope. If anyone had asked me, "Hey, are you a Christian?" I would have said, "Sure, I guess so." God was a set of ideas that my father had given me like a hand-me-down wardrobe; God was always someone else's passion, a small sound in the background of my noisy world, a foul-weather friend on whom I rarely called. I hadn't been to church since I left my parents' house, and prayers were not a part of my Day-Timer schedule. I was just too busy being twenty, and then being thirty, a wife, a mother, a worker, a doer, who thought of her soul about as often as she thought of her socks. I was just gliding along until your death stopped me, and I paused long enough to ask, "What am I doing?" and I looked at my spirit, hanging limp at the back of my closet. I saw in its silvery threads the meaning I had been missing. I saw in its origins the shadowy hand of God himself.

Slowly, and quite painfully at times, I looked at the issue of God from all sides. I tried on the shoulder-shrug of agnosticism, but found it didn't suit me; I needed to take a stand. I considered the possibility that there was no God, and that the afterlife was merely a wild concoction of our panic-stricken minds. For the first time, I reflected on religion as an antidote to fear, the creation of human beings all bent on denying the permanence of death. It was in this mind space that I vacationed, off and on, for a year or more. It was a sphere where life held no meaning beyond its physical stimulations and material gains; it was a realm whose most fitting motto might be "So what?" and whose absence of gravity, of genuine purpose, made effortful living seem silly and obsolete. It was cold there, Mark, and empty as a mollusk's shell.

Ultimately, it didn't make sense. Look at the intricacies of our universe, the complexities of our existence, the singular detail and synchrony of nature's vast kingdom, and then try to imagine it all as the outgrowth of simple cells dividing crazily in some primordial ooze. Left unexplained by the atheist's view are everyday miracles, near-death experiences, supernatural phenomena, human love, our hungering for purpose, our glaring uniqueness on a planet occupied by instinct-driven animals and dull-witted insects. Why is it that other species have not evolved as far as humans have? How is it that nature has created something more intelligent than itself? The questions go on and on, and they all seem to have the same answer.

As a thoughtful, discerning person, I eventually came back to God. After all my searching and prodding, all my investigative reading and philosophical hunting, there could be no denying his existence. I felt as if something had happened to me, Mark, and something had. There is a significant difference between the mere inheritance of faith and its miraculous, hard-fought discovery, alive and pulsing, in one's own heart; the experience is distinct, illuminating, life-giving, and life-changing. It is as difficult to describe as God's own grace.

Am I deliriously faithful all the time? No. Do I find myself occasionally afflicted with doubt? Yes, of course. Experiencing one's spirit, feeding one's soul, coming to know God, is not a static situation but a flowing one, a maddening flux of faith and skepticism, joy and frustration. But it is a struggle that matters. It is fraught with meaning. It is a trek that makes life purposeful, intentional, worth all its effort and travails and up-and-down phases.

It is paradoxical, unjust, bittersweet, Mark, that it took the ending of your life here to bring about the real beginning of mine. But I like to think that we both experienced a birth of sorts, that we shared yet another grand adventure, that we each discovered life all over again where we least expected to find it.

With love from here to there,

M

Chapter 7

Memorandum to My Muse...

"When I take my hands off the
steering wheel and my
eyes off the road,
there is finally an opportunity
for you do your mystical,
gifted driving."

.

Memorandum to My Muse . . .

TO: My Muse
FROM: MMK
RE: Creativity, Work, and Lessons Learned the Hard Way

Let me say first of all, Muse, that I'm not really sure who you are. Neither do I know how you live, or where, or why your route, like the milkman's, seems to include my house on some days but definitely not on others. You are perhaps a creative vapor, you are most certainly a mystery, and you rarely show up when I call. An exasperating mix, indeed.

Popularly, you have always been characterized as an arbitrary and madness-provoking creature who lives apart from us humans. Artists of all stripes know you, and yet they don't. You are the giver of ideas, the inspirer, the one who finishes novels and salvages paintings when the artist has exhausted all avenues and lost all hope. But even as you play in our midst, you are enveloped in darkness, ethereal as the gifts you bring, wholly unpredictable and permanently, outrageously, out of our reach. A generous benefactor one day, you are a miser the next.

There have been times when a wonderful idea has appeared in my mind only to fall into total ruin on the page. Other times have found me stymied, wordless, hunkered over paper as blank and motionless as the stream of my thoughts. I am there, ready to work, but you are not. I wait around for you as I would for a bus, but eventually I stalk away in disgust, stood up once again.

But there are other occasions when you show up, unannounced, unexpected, and do my work for me. Like a secretary taking dictation, I simply write down the melodic sentences you weave on your loom; it feels like a dream or a thrilling downhill ride. You come into my mind, you take over, and then you exit before the lights come up. At the close of one of your visits, I am left exhilarated, tired, and vaguely guilty, like a student who passed a test only because a classmate furtively supplied the answers. I present the work as my own but don't always feel I have a right to.

Because I am human, and because I love to have hard work made easy, I court you shamelessly. I want you to come and sit alongside me on a full-time basis. Together, we could become a writer of some note without the usual anguish and discipline, without all that arduous labor and excavation of the soul. If I could only figure out the combination, I might open up your vaulted wisdom and make it my own. You see, Muse, I want to have some control in this relationship of ours, but I can't seem to gain so much as an ounce of it.

If I could have some small amount of authority, I might ask you to adapt your schedule to mine. You know that I have children, and that I have only a couple of hours each day to work; still, you come whenever it suits you. Rather than arriving promptly at 8:30 when I am poised over my computer keyboard, you show you up at half past three when I'm poised over a sink full of dishes or a Monopoly board dotted with threatening hotels. It's always when I'm reading a book or wielding a dust rag or doing something, anything, that does not pertain to writing that you appear with a provocative notion or a fully formed sentence. I dutifully drop whatever I'm doing and scramble off to record the idea, looking for all the world like a person with an extremely short attention span or a precarious mental state.

It is my theory, Muse, that you are deliberately hanging back, waiting, and that your timing reflects a brilliance I have foolishly overlooked. It seems entirely possible that you come on a schedule designed not to be inconvenient, but to be unlimited by the constraints of my earthbound timetable. You will not be corralled by my frivolous demands. And, more important, you will not come until I get out of your way.

Perhaps you arrive when I'm mopping or daydreaming or scanning the headlines because it is at these times that my overbusy intellect shifts into a less ambitious gear. I'm not trying to squeeze out ideas like toothpaste from a tube. I'm not rifling through my mental word file looking for the perfect verb. I'm not trying to inflict myself on the creative process, to batter and cajole it, until it bends to my whim. When I take my hands off the steering wheel and my eyes off the road, there is finally an opportunity for you to do your mystical, gifted driving.

It is not an opportunity you consistently seize, though. Mostly, you leave me to my own devices and let me wrestle with concepts and moan and rewrite and give up four or five times until, at last, I learn. It is when I finally learn something from the work that I finally have something to say, and it is when I have something real to say that the words flow out of me like long-denied tears.

Last night I saw a television interview with the magnificent Toni Morrison, a writer you must know well, Muse. She seemed to believe that inspiration is nothing more, and nothing less, than hard work. Maybe that's true and I've been chasing after a mirage. Maybe these tasks of ours are meant to be difficult. Little is learned from the easy and illusory, but much is made known through the tough and the hardscrabble and the laboriously earned. If it is my job to learn from this process, then I suppose it has to be painful at times, tedious, challenging, and occasionally, gloriously, simple, even joyful now and then.

So what have I learned today, Muse? Only that you will help me if I let you, and that I might experience more personal growth when you choose not to. I've seen value in the struggle, and a side of myself that sometimes prefers bliss to insight, a free ride to a long walk. I've noticed that the creative process, with its manic highs and cavernous lows, mirrors life, and that this same creative process, this learning process, is life itself. And I've realized something else too. You, Muse, seem a lot like another benevolent figure I've worked with, a force of love, a sacred provider, who helps me when I let him and who wants me to know struggle so that I might also know wisdom.

Maybe, old friend, I know who you are after all.

Chapter 8

Dear Matthew,

"It is simply the story of you,
a boy once made
distinctive by an inclination
to pull inward,
closer to himself and further
from the world, and of me,
a mother who grudgingly
confronted her fears
and some parts of herself
she preferred not to see."

Dear Matthew,

This is not a letter you should read today, as you begin third grade and your year of being eight. In this letter are chapters of your history which you don't remember and which I've never fully illustrated for you; it has occurred to me that too much knowledge about your early life could color your self-view in the present, as a red sweater bleeds in the wash to make everything around it pink. Maybe when you are a bit older, your identity will be solid enough to tolerate a little re-touching of those old toddler snapshots.

I don't mean to raise your expectations for some shocking family scandal. There are no alternative parents claiming you as their own, no strange sagas of alien abduction or inbred madness.

It is nothing so grand or sensational as that. It is simply the story of you, a boy once made distinctive by an inclination to pull inward, closer to himself and further from the world, and of me, a mother who grudgingly confronted her fears and some parts of herself she preferred not to see.

I've told you stories about your babyhood—the lurch and reel of your too-young digestive system, the window seat in our old house where we sat and watched the trees sway, the sound of your crib toys calling out like roosters in the morning—but it was later, around the age of two, when this rosy picture began to yellow around the edges.

Your ability to learn and use words was not developing. Those few words that did come were repeated and enjoyed for a week or so, and then put away forever like outgrown toys. Everyone reassured me that boys are slower to blossom, that you would, in your own time, begin to speak, and I was eager to believe them.

As you approached the age of three, what speech you had was sing-songy and largely unintelligible to everyone but me. You consistently reversed the pronouns "you" and "I," echoed my words but seemed not to know what they meant, had obvious trouble following verbal instructions. You showed an unusual talent for decoding printed words, though; you memorized car logos and could identify every one as we walked through a parking lot. I remember when we took a Gymboree class, all the other kids were playing on the gym equipment and you were walking around the room reading the Gymboree logos stenciled on the wall.

Your doctor was not especially impressed by all this. We went in for a regular checkup and, as he asked you questions and you offered no responses, I filled the silence with my practiced explanations. Citing your history of ear infections, the doctor referred us to a hearing specialist. He thought you might be hearing-impaired; I gamely agreed to investigate and then cried as we drove the route home. It was too much for me that day to consider that something might be wrong with you. It was a terrible thing to have my fears confirmed by another, to have them brought out and examined like dirty little secrets. I began to mourn the potential loss of "normal" and to cautiously circle the concept of "different."

One test led to another and another, and soon you were enrolled in a special-education class for children with speech delays and serious articulation errors. Your hearing was fine, they said. It was something else that stood in your way, something obstinate and unidentified, something essentially unknowable that occupied your mind like an unwanted houseguest.

It wasn't long before the teachers called me for another conference. As it turned out, your problems were not restricted to speech. They told me you couldn't be relied upon to follow along in a single-file line; you would frequently veer off into your own airspace instead of turning a corner with the rest of the class. You couldn't process verbal requests. There was a marked aversion for other kids; you could not tolerate having someone play beside you, much less with you. It was the teachers' recommendation that you be reassigned to a "multi-needs" program where your classmates would include children living with Down's syndrome, autism, and profounder brands of mental retardation. It meant very little to you, this change in direction, but it meant a great deal to me. An ache grew up within me, so deep, so unrelenting, it was as if my soul had been scraped and sculpted by the blade of a knife.

I remember feeling afraid for you. I kept thinking, Matthew, about the cruelty of the world, its abject intolerance of people who are different, slower, unable to move with the heavy traffic streaming toward success. I imagined the taunting and social rejection you might experience, the separateness you might feel, the subtle recognition that no place had been reserved for you at life's best tables. Every single hurt I had known in my own history, all the painful reproaches and quiet refusals and picked-last humiliations of my long-gone playground years, revisited my dreams. Only this time it was you who suffered, my firstborn son, one of the greatest, most consuming loves of my life, the one who I would protect and cherish beyond all reasonable limit. It was you, Matthew, and I could not bear it. I wanted to make your life perfect, to renovate and decorate it as I would an old, abandoned house, but the door was locked. I couldn't fix it for you. I couldn't make it right.

You were oblivious to all of this, of course, as a three-year-old who transmitted and received few signals. I suspected that this might not always be the case, however. Someday, you might want a place of your own, a job, a grown-up life that you may or may not be able to manage by yourself. As no real progress was registered in that first special-ed. year and the teachers and I began to tiptoe around the word "autistic," I forced myself to look at a picture of the future where nothing had really changed, where you interacted with us but much preferred the universe of you, where you might work in some menial position that involved counting or sorting or labeling, something outside the public eye. The idea that you would probably never have a fulfilling career or a chance to race on the big track saddened me tremendously and sometimes made me angry; it irritated me that our society could be so competitive and merciless as to shut out those who are not perfectly packaged. To you I presented a supportive and affectionate countenance, but behind my smile I was ceaselessly sorry for you.

At some point in the midst of all my pity for you and myself, God sent me an angel in the form of a supermarket bagboy. He was about twenty years old, I would guess, and he was working outside on a blustery afternoon collecting carts from the parking lot. I was loading groceries into my trunk when he came over and began to help me. He had a lot to say, this boy. He had just purchased a new Pontiac Firebird and it was this jubilant subject he wanted to discuss and review and exalt to his heart's content. His pride was palpable, his joy as plain as sunlight. But as he began to reiterate points he had illuminated just moments before, as I mentally made note of the fact that this boy was "slow," functional and yet somehow not, probably condemned to a series of unrewarding jobs, I began to feel sorry for him too. I pitied him for being a square knob in our world of perfect roundness.

As these thoughts flowed through my mind, though, he continued to talk, to be happy and proud and wholly satisfied with the life that was uniquely his. He was not pitiable to himself, only to me; he clearly liked his job and he did it well. He arrived there at the store each day, where he was known and needed, in a new car he bought for himself. I realized that he was probably happier than I was, and the problem I thought was his actually belonged to me.

It finally dawned on me in that cold, November parking lot that it was not just our culture that turned an indifferent eye on those who could not keep up, it was me. I was the one who was too perfectionistic, overly competitive, ever impatient with that which was irregular or a pace or two behind. It was me who had decided, while you were age three and completely unaware of my dismal predictions and utter faithlessness, that your life would be meaningless, monotonous, without gladness or direction, simply because it would be different from mine. It was shame that overcame me then, rushing all around me like a frigid coastal tide. The lesson I learned was as hard and unforgiving as my own thoughtless judgments.

Was this humbling and transformational lesson the reason God sent you to me in the first place? I don't know, Matthew. But I believe it was through God's grace and infinite mercy that you were quietly coaxed away from the quasi-autistic destination toward which you had been walking so intently. In the next year, when you were four, everything changed. It was a miracle. You opened up, layer by layer, like a complex, exotic flower. You talked and talked and talked, and made a few tentative friendships. Just as I learned to accept you as you were, you became something else, and my work began anew.

My work is never quite over, though. In spite of your complete metamorphosis, your academic excellence, your active social life, we still encounter bumps in the road that I wish were not there. Your temper can be blistering. Schoolwork is sometimes approached with casual slapdashery. You are terribly hard on your brother, Matthew. Sometimes I find myself trying to perfect you, sanding your faults, chiseling at them, trying to change their colors or disguise them as "phases." I pray for greater patience and a more accepting nature. I remind myself that you are you, cantankerous, stubborn, a cognitive gymnast, and I am me, impatient, restless, and forever struggling with a million weaknesses of my own.

Live your life fully, Matthew, and make it your own. You have taught me that being our imperfect, human selves is the only thing we can do perfectly.

All my love,

Mom

Chapter 9

Dear God,

"Perhaps I have come to terms
with doubt because I finally
understand it as an
essential ingredient
of faith."

Dear God,

This is not my traditional style of speaking to you, yet it seems fitting that a writer should occasionally write to the one who made her a writer in the first place. I suppose this is not so much a prayer as it is a story or a rumination or a string of thoughts that will transcend convention and settle peaceably between us. You know what I mean to say before I even say it, but I take comfort in laying my thoughts out on paper, like a baker sets pies out to cool on a window sill.

I think the time has finally come in this journey of mine where I can face my doubts about you, examine them closely, and then tuck them away in the small interior closet where they will likely live on, in one form or another, for the rest of my days. They no longer scare me. I have learned to live with the idea that not all puzzles are handily solved, not all mystery is meant to be boiled down to dull logic. Perhaps I have come to terms with doubt because I finally understand it as an essential ingredient of faith.

You know, Lord, that I have struggled against doubt for a few years now and it has felt like a crisis of faith. I always believed that its presence within me rendered faith impossible. It seemed to me that your steadfast followers were sure of you in a way that I could not be, and I envied them. But faith would not be faith without the possibility of error or misjudgment; if faith represented certainty, it would not be faith, but fact. "Fact" is a term we assign to things we feel we have thoroughly mastered, whether through study, scientific experimentation, or objective consideration—it implies resolution and certitude and a degree of human dominion. But faith is different. Faith is mysterious, ambiguous, emotional. It requires much more of us than the grasping of facts; it demands that we apply ourselves to it daily, that our minds and hearts and souls be engaged in it, that we swim against the popular tides of skepticism and suspicion. Faith requires that we risk being wrong, while fact allows us to be perpetually right.

It was the riskiness of faith, and its inherently active nature, that scared me most, I think. I have always preferred the solid, bulky feel of life's great trunk over the shaky sensation of its more harrowing limbs. I am forever on the trail of safe choices, though in a passive, wait-and-see fashion that is both cautious and comfortable. The rigors of faith challenged my system; there would be a commitment involved, I was sure, and a stepping-out from the shadows, an endless pursuit of spiritual wisdom, a delving into my character, an ethical influence on my choices in life, that would be decidedly less comfortable than doing nothing at all. So I sat on my couch and awaited some proof. I wanted my faith to be based in fact, and thus not to be faith at all.

Proof of your existence would make it easy, Lord. A fiery show in the sky, an apparition of Mary, angels walking in daylight—any of these things would render my decision to follow you simple. Concrete evidence would remove risk from the equation like sun will lift fog from the land. There would be no reason to waffle, no excuse for hesitation, if only I had something tangible to hold on to. I prayed for miracles, for signs, and I waited a while longer. On some level, Lord, I think I wanted you to carry me over the prickly brambles of doubt rather than taking those steps on my own.

In spite of your eternally forgiving nature, I imagine it is painful when those you have created question your existence in much the same way they might question the claims of a candidate for mayor. We are a suspicious lot, here on earth. Credibility and trust have vanished from our midst like yesterday's styles. Truth is in short supply, and it's hard to recognize. We've all been fooled, Lord, lied to by people we trusted, manipulated, suckered, made to feel that, on the whole, nothing is as it appears to be. There is a cynicism that lives among us, and we use it as the ancient warriors once used their mighty shields.

Though I am not knowledgeable about the Bible, I know that credibility was a problem even in the days when Jesus lived on earth. Many people adopted the popular posture that he was crazy or criminal or hungry for control. It was a courageous act then for Christ's disciples to choose belief over skepticism, just as it is now. They had to separate themselves from the safety of the doubting throng, draw unwelcome attention to themselves, face the possibility of social isolation and even death. They had to take risks, even though it was easier not to.

I am beginning to understand, Lord, that faith was never intended to be an easy proposition. All commitments, whether human or divine, require faith, and no commitment of a serious caliber evolves through a superficial or effortless process. Acquaintances do not become cherished friends overnight, husbands do not typically marry their wives on the day they first meet. We spend time with each other, learn about one another, examine both the good and the not-so-good in our mosaic human personas, and then we make a choice to either have faith in that person or move on. When we marry or buy a new house, we take a calculated risk, a leap of faith, because we cannot know for sure that our judgments are neither clouded by emotion nor greased with subconscious agendas. There are no guarantees, no certificates of proof, that things or people are what they claim to be. But we take the risk anyway, because our need for love and security and comfort, both material and spiritual, occasionally supersedes our need to protect ourselves, our need to be right.

I don't mean to suggest that choosing to follow you, Lord, is like choosing a spouse or a new set of clothes. It is far more sacred than anything here on earth. But I come to the choice as a person of the earth, one who has made plenty of mistakes and would like to make no more, one who finds the firm textures of fact and tangibility easier, safer, than the mysterious folds of faith and spirit.

But as I weighed the merits of believing versus agnosticism, it occurred to me that the arguments against belief are no more real or convincing or concrete than faith itself. I realized, too, that much of what matters in life remains unproven. There is no proof that the human spirit exists, or hope or love, except that we feel the wonder of these things within us, we feel their effects on our lives. I have never thought to question the existence of joy or peace or compelling intuition, and never have I awaited evidence of their reality. Some things are simply felt, simply known. The proof of their existence is a phenomenon, an experience, that cannot be seen or heard or properly described. And so it is with you, Father.

I see now that I have believed in things I could not prove or measure since my time here began. Love is a vapor, hope is a dream, and yet they rule my life. I feel them, just as I sometimes feel your presence. If ever again I question your existence (and I imagine I will, however fleetingly, however regrettably), I will think of the awesome power of devotion and its pitiful lack of evidence. I will think of the magnetic energy of ideas and their utter formlessness in the physical world. I will not ask for proof again, nor wait for any miracles. On most days you are simply known to me, Lord, and so is my faith in you, and that is miracle enough.

With praise and gratitude,

M

Chapter 10

Dear Scott,

"The passage of an anniversary
brings with it an
urge to look back,
to retrace the steps that
led us from then to now,
to run our hands over the
rippled surface of our
life together,
admiring the texture,
checking for leaks."

Dear Scott,

In a few weeks we'll be celebrating our tenth wedding anniversary, and I find myself in a nostalgic mood. The passage of an anniversary brings with it an urge to look back, to retrace the steps that led us from then to now, to run our hands over the rippled surface of our life together, admiring the texture, checking for leaks. We are older, of course, far wiser than when we met; we understand now what it means to be married. And yet we have stayed together, in spite of ourselves, in spite of the "me" and "you" that sometimes resist, sometimes embrace, the nebulous boundaries of "we."

You and I each came to our marriage with our young-adult

selfishness in full flower; we were both in our late twenties, professionals with apartments of our own, immersed for some years in that magical me-space where clothes left in heaps on the floor are never remarked upon, never noticed, never the subject of prickly dialogues. We each came and went as we pleased, kept our own odd hours, ate popcorn for breakfast if we felt like it, and stayed in the shower until all the hot water was gone.

You and I had plenty of time to become set in our ways before we found ourselves mixed up in each other's lives, before the day came when I suddenly found myself pausing to consider how you might feel about Lean Cuisines for dinner, how my desire to see a movie might conflict with your desire to watch football, how my excessively long weekend sleep patterns were now interrupted by you, a man who got up early even if it was Saturday, even if there was no reason whatsoever to leave the bed's intoxicating warmth. It wasn't just "me" anymore. Now there was "you," too. Without our express consent and without our full awareness, we had become "we."

In spite of those heady years of rugged individualism, you and I fell into we-ness with very little sacrifice. I had to get rid of my cat, Rachel, because her presence caused your eyes to itch and swell like big, fat mosquito bites; it hurt to see her go, but I don't recall the decision to give her to my mother as particularly difficult. We wisely chose an apartment with two bathrooms so there would be no squabbles in the morning. We spent a lot of time with your friends, but I liked them; soon enough, they were my friends too. The whole we-thing was so novel, and made so exhilarating by the heart-first spin of new love, that we tumbled into it without hesitation, without the usual reluctance of over-thinking adults. We were like the little kids we see at the pool each summer, who fling themselves off the diving board even though they're not really sure they can swim.

Before our second wedding anniversary arrived, and before the new-car smell had completely left our marriage, our first son was born. It was at this juncture, I think, that the concept of "we" was expanded beyond the point of all reason. Now, both our lives were run by the squalling objections of a very small person who ate constantly, who routinely and emphatically soiled diapers and linens, and who charmed us into thinking that we really didn't need sleep after all. In the short span of three years, we had traveled from the land of self-centered singlehood to the twilight zone existence of new parenthood.

I can't speak for you, honey, but by the time our second son was born, I had lost touch with me-hood altogether. I had melded myself into the family unit thoroughly and without conscious thought; it was easy, even delightful, to meet the needs that you and the boys scattered across my days like buckets full of Lego's. I think it was enough for me then to be so obviously needed, so depended upon, so central to the welfare of three people I loved much more than I could ever love a great book or a long nap or a brilliant literary career. The "me" I once knew lay freeze-dried, indefinitely postponed, beneath a blanket of family responsibility I had gladly put there myself.

But then, a couple of years ago, things began to change. I don't know if it was the onset of marital monotony, or the fact that the kids didn't need me as acutely as they once did, or the sudden realization that my life would not go on forever, but I found myself wrestling with needs of my own again. My meness was reasserting itself, like the sun pushing its way through a dense layer of clouds.

At first, it was subtle. I began making time for books and movies and female friendships. I accepted fewer of the freelance business writing assignments that had, over the years, become a source of stress and tedium. I started to exercise more control over how my time was spent. Finally, I had a few spare minutes for contemplation and reflection, and I wasn't pleased with the life I was reflecting on. Somehow, I had forgotten all about my dreams and goals, what I believed to be my purpose here, and now I was reminded. A deep yearning for new forms of fulfillment rose up within me; it was then that I set about discovering where this unexpected wave of spiritual longing might lead.

It wasn't an effortless process. I know that I have not been easy to live with these past couple of years. Preoccupied, frustrated at times, learning to set limits and to be more vocal about my needs, I expected more and more of you. Without explicitly asking for it, I awaited your permission to redefine the focus of my life, and when you didn't give it to me, I became irritated. I wanted you to draw a map and plan my itinerary; still entangled in the engaging web of we-ness, I failed to understand that this was a journey I had to direct for myself.

As I look back on this period of personal growth, Scott, I feel relieved, emancipated, full of joyful resolve. I have finally found the courage to write my own stories instead of someone else's. There is a spiritual tone to my life that wasn't there before, and a faith in God's grace that has been inwardly transformational. I feel more full than empty, more found than lost. But I can't help feeling a little bit scared too. From the beginning of this remodeling project, I have been harboring the quiet but persistent fear that you won't love the "me" that now exists just outside of "we."

At times, I have asked myself if I've gone too far, if I've changed so much that we are no longer aboard the same train, no longer headed for the same destination. I wonder if the weness of our marriage can tolerate all this self-realization. I look at you some days and I wonder if you feel that I'm pulling away from you, pulling too hard at the fabric of "us."

Whatever doubts you've had are seldom expressed. An occasional crinkle in your forehead or a tilt to your eyebrows sends a silent signal that my restless, seeking nature is a little foreign to you. You don't claim to consistently understand me, but you have consistently supported me as I've tried to understand myself. You have perhaps even freeze-dried and indefinitely postponed "you," setting yourself aside gladly until my growing pains subside. You have been precisely the "you" I needed in order to go looking for "me."

So this is the seesaw accommodation of marriage, the reconciliation of needs that makes possible the existence of separate selves within the province of "us." I guess the marital "we" is not a giving up of selves, but simply a giving of them, one to the other and back again.

Thanks for your patience, honey, and happy anniversary.

Love,

M

Chapter 11

Dear Mary,

"It is a hard business,
this closure of friendship. . . .
We feel as if we have done
something wrong,
failed at something important."

Dear Mary,

I t must come as a great surprise, this letter, since we have not
spoken in twelve years or so. The last time I remember calling you was when I became officially engaged to be married;
there was no answer. Time elapsed, our lives moved forward. I
sent you an announcement after our Key West wedding (an
elopement, really, since no one else was there), but, again, there
was no answer. More years came and went, more silence, and so
ended a friendship that spanned at least a decade, an entire era
of youth and reluctant, new adulthood.

Obviously, there is more to the story. We didn't stop being
friends because of a couple of missed connections, or because of
some minor misunderstanding. It cannot be blamed on any

singular event, a bitter argument or a stinging betrayal. No such thing occurred. Rather, there was a slow, imperceptible drift, a parting of interests and lifestyles and conversational leanings that bleached the color in our friendship to a lighter, less remarkable hue. Where we once seemed so compatible, we gradually took note of our differences; though we started our walk from the same corner, we found ourselves, years later, on opposite sides of town.

We met, as I remember it, as juniors in high school. Though we had known of each other for some time, it wasn't until eleventh grade that we entered into the same social orbit. My new boyfriend was one of your closest buddies. Naturally, you and I began to turn up at the same parties and hangouts. We were both seventeen, from similar families in similar towns, and now we had friends in common. We became friends ourselves as easily, as thoughtlessly, as children join hands when crossing the street.

In many ways, we were a perfect match. We balanced each other: You were bolder, louder, more of a leader than me, and I was your irreverent, though bashful, sidekick. You were an organizer of parties, a girl who knew where things were happening or made them happen herself. Blessed with a dominant personality, you orchestrated the workings of our social circle like a queen bee runs her humming hive.

Encumbered with a passive, uncertain nature, I drank in your confidence. I was attracted by your style and repelled by my own. Like Ed McMahon, I was content to chortle from the sidelines and set up your jokes as long as I could be warmed by the broad beam of your unbounded self-assurance.

We were in sync, two hands on a ticking clock, until I left for college the year after we met. Though we remained friends and spent time together during my college hiatuses, it was during that period, I believe, that the first split appeared in the seam of our relationship. Maybe it was the geographic separation. Perhaps the interruption of our momentum came a little too soon. Or possibly, we were growing up and beginning to change.

I graduated and returned from college, and then promptly left again; this time, I said good-bye to our mild, suburban village and took an apartment on the north side of Chicago. While I was still trying to figure out who I might want to date, you got married; a year or two later, your first child was born. The two girls whose lives had been so similar now lived in separate towns and, from a lifestyle perspective, in foreign nations. You were a conscientious wife and mother, and I was an unsettled woman whose life focused mainly on smart career moves and hot, smoky nightclubs. Suddenly, gradually, all we really had in common was a piece of shared history, a time we remembered when things had been different, when we looked at each other and saw parts of ourselves, when the thoughts and wishes of one validated, celebrated, the dreams of the other.

Our lives had changed, Mary, and so had our characters. As I became more and more sure of myself, more willing to take risks and run my own life, our time-honored dynamic—you lead, I follow—began to chafe. The yoke of our relationship, which we had each agreed to wear, no longer seemed to be the right shape or size. We tried to adjust it, to wait out the difficulties, but ultimately, painfully, we surrendered our hold on the past, on each other, and set off in our respective new directions.

It is a hard business, this closure of friendship. It is a lot like divorce, or death, but there are no legal rituals or solemn ceremonies to mark it. We feel as though we have done something wrong, failed at something important. But to assume that we have failed is to assume too that friendships are only "successful" if they last forever, if the members of it weather change, or resist it so effectively that the bonds we forge at age ten or twenty still fit like gloves at forty. When you think of it, it seems a little unrealistic for us to expect our friendships to endure through eternity, to stay intact when everything else about us and around us is swirling and transforming.

But, I imagine, that is exactly what we do expect when we are well within the heady thrall of a close friendship. We feel so utterly taken care of, so marvelously supported and understood, that we fall effortlessly into the "friends forever" dream. We cannot fathom that this wonderful bond would ever change its dimensions or come untied. But it occurs to me now that some friendships may actually crumble under the burden of those very expectations, under the ungainly hope, the impossible wish, that things will always stay just as they are right now. From relationships and people that are inherently changeable, evolving, en route from one place to another, we look for sameness, stability, and the comforting glow of permanence.

Eventually, inevitably, things happen, other relationships encroach, small shifts occur. Our high expectations of one another are not fully met, or are not met in the way to which we've grown accustomed. It is then that we feel the beginnings of pain, fear, and a desperate sense of impending loss; the forever-ness we had counted on begins to look a little shaky. Subtly, we start to view the changing friendship, the slipping-away friend, with a critical, unsparing eye, a less charitable heart, the heavy shadings of acute disappointment. Petty grievances grow large. Unreturned phone calls are weighted with meaning. We feel as though we have been betrayed, and we have—not by the friend, but by our own too-big ideas of what the friend, the friendship, should always and forever be.

Maybe, Mary, if we'd been a little more flexible, a little more willing to bend with the changes in our lives and their impact on who we are, both apart and together, we would still be friends. But it would be different than it once was, because we are different. And as much as it would have changed already, it would change yet again. We would have to forgive each other for constantly growing, developing, moving on to divergent life stages, and we would have to forgive ourselves for mourning, for missing, the way it used to be.

It wasn't a forever friendship, Mary, but it was a meaningful one. It was successful, in spite of its conclusion. We got some things wrong, but we also got a lot of them right. I wish things could have been different; I wish, in some ways, things could have stayed the same. I still think about you, and I wish you well on the many roads you've already chosen and on those you have yet to discover. I can say with all certainty, Mary, that the roads I've chosen since we parted have been subtly tinted, subtly altered, from the singular experience of knowing you. Maybe ours was some other kind of forever thing, each of us having left an indelible print, a lasting impression, on the rim of the other's soul.

Love,

M

Chapter 12

Dear Grandma and Grandpa,

"You showed me there was
another way to live,
a way unlike my parents',
and I believe it was your
tender example that saved me
from becoming another
kind of woman
in another kind of life."

Dear Grandma and Grandpa,

When I think of you, as I often do, I love to remember you in your apartment above the dry cleaner's downtown. You lived there more than twenty years, I'm sure, and that place means a great deal to me, because it was yours, and because I can't go there anymore. Your apartment appears in my dreams on a regular basis and in many of them, I walk through the door to find your world intact. It is as if you have merely stepped out for a moment, and not for all eternity; it still looks the same, and the kitchen still smells faintly of bananas, and it feels like home. There is a strong thread of safety and contentedness embroidered into the rugs and old-fashioned chairs, the folded bath towels and collections of hats.

I wonder sometimes if you ever had an inkling of your importance to me; I didn't fully realize it myself until our era together ended. You were wonderful grandparents in the traditional sense, but there was much more to it than that. The two of you offered me solace and comfort, a place where I could be a child and lay my defenses to rest in the skylit hallway outside your door. In your company, in your kitchen, I could postpone my worries and misplace my anxieties as if on a tropical vacation. I could forget, for an hour or two, about the unstable atmosphere at home.

I'm sure you suspected something was wrong. Living just a mile or two from our house, you saw and heard things that others might miss; you two were our frequent baby-sitters, so you were there when my parents came home drunk and testy. Dropping in unannounced, you might have seen bruises shaped like continents spread across my mother's skin. On holidays, my Dad's inner turmoil would begin to darken his countenance, spoil his thoughts, as the day wore on and olives piled up at the bottom of his martini glass. I know he used to call you at night, drunk, and go on and on about things. It's okay now, Grandma and Grandpa, to acknowledge that you had an idea about the alcohol and violence. It's okay to say it, to let the secret out.

I imagine it was hard for you, knowing about the troubles but not being able to stop them. It was not fashionable at the time, nor a part of your characters, to intervene and cause a big commotion. But you did do something. For me, and probably for Mom and Dad and Todd, you performed a thousand wordless favors, a raft of kind deliveries. Like a pair of God's own angels, you hovered around us and offered your hands when we needed to be held. You were available to us, every day and in the dead of night.

I can remember only a few times when I went to your apartment and you weren't there. Mostly, I would drop in after school or in the midst of a trip through town, and surprise you. The door was never locked. Grandpa would be baking cookies or napping in his chair by the window. You, Grandma, were hosting a bridge party or talking on the phone, polishing silver or running the vacuum. Figurines and little knickknacks sat steadily in their places, and the clock in the dining room chimed on the hour. If it was lunchtime, "As the World Turns" was on, and two sandwiches would be laid out on the red cardtable. Sometimes, I would come in and find the two of you having a laugh together, flirting a little; Grandma would swat at you with her dishtowel, Grandpa, as if she were mad, and then you would both giggle, tickled still by this familiar old routine.

What would I have done without this place of quiet love? How might I have endured the pain and chaos of home without you? I often wonder. You see, Grandma and Grandpa, you were my refuge. I knew there would be no yelling at your house, no fists raised in anger, no loud noises crashing through my sleep like trucks full of granite. There was no possibility of injury there, no chance for trembling and tears and eyewitness agony. The only thing that happened there was an afternoon game of gin rummy, and the simple expression of your hearts and minds. You showed me there was another way to live, a way unlike my parents', and I believe it was your tender example that saved me from becoming another kind of woman in another kind of life.

You rescued me. I am thinking now of a night in 1972 when I was fourteen. Dad and I had eaten dinner at your place because Mom was out somewhere. I don't know if Dad was just in a combative mood, or if he'd had too many drinks that evening, but I remember the conversation turned sour. It was spring break, and Dad had earlier given me permission to go out that night with my friends. But in the angry, arbitrary style of his after-dark persona, he abruptly ruled that no such thing would occur. I probably tried to reason with him, and I think you did too. But he was determined to stick with his choice, in spite of its punitive nature, in spite of its utter groundlessness, and we left your place in a cloud of emotion.

When we got home, Dad went down to the basement and I rashly decided to run away. Following in the footsteps of my older brother, I snuck out of the house and went to meet my friends. I remember running through people's yards, trying to stay off the street in case Dad came looking for me. I felt liberated, but a chill sense of dread rampaged through my system like a mean, aggressive virus.

It turned out to be a pretty dull evening with my friends; there was nothing special going on and soon enough, everyone had to meet their curfews. It hadn't occurred to me that I would wind up alone in the middle of the night, afraid to go home, wandering around, cold, with nowhere to go. I hadn't thought that far ahead but, as it turned out, you had.

I found out later that Dad had begun calling you, at fifteen-minute intervals, as soon as he realized I was missing. He was apparently drinking heavily as he waited for me, and his rage was building. Not only was he convinced I would come to your apartment, but he was evidently convinced that you wouldn't tell him I was there; so he called and he called and he called. As I've been told, Grandpa, you finally hung up on him. You were a reserved man who had perhaps slammed a door only once in your life, but you stood up to my dad on my behalf, and the very thought of it still brings tears to my eyes.

It must have been well after midnight when I came to the sidewalk beneath your windows. I can't tell you how surprised and relieved I was to see that all the lights were on. You were waiting for me, and you turned on all the lights so I would know it. You stayed up, hours after your customary bedtime, because you thought I might need you. And I did. I really needed you that night, and you were there to greet me at the door. I can't remember a time when I felt more understood, or more loved, than when I found you waiting there.

We talked a while, as I recall, and then Grandma said, "We'll go and face the music," and we did. You drove me home. Dad had already passed out. Mom was awake and more than a little annoyed about having come home to find a runaway drama in progress. I suppose we all wearily went to our respective beds after that, and I'm fairly sure I was grounded for the rest of my spring break.

But I'm not sure, Grandma and Grandpa, if I ever thanked you. Caught up as I was in the anguish of the moment, I may have forgotten. I may have forgotten a hundred other times too to tell you what you meant to me. Please accept this letter, belatedly, as a symbol of my love and gratitude. I thank you for your steadiness, your loyalty, your particular brand of love without conditions. And I thank God for giving me you, my grandma and grandpa, my angels, who are still hovering around me, who are somewhere waiting for me even now, with all the lights aglow.

With great love,

M

Chapter 13

Dear Miss Vesta,

"In all the gray and troubled
years of my adolescence,
when pimples and boyfriends came
and went and I nearly failed
both algebra and geometry,
my father always reminded
me of what you said,
and he spoke of my career,
my calling, as if it were a
story he had seen in a
thousand different dreams."

Dear Miss Vesta,

There was a talent show, and I danced in my toe shoes in front of the whole class; most of the boys laughed, but one of them, Guy Ryan, whom I would love for the rest of elementary school, did not. On another day, Denny Crebs punched me; I punched him back, and we were both sent to sit on chairs in the hallway. There were multiplication tables lining the walls of our room like long, ancient scrolls. This is what I remember, Miss Vesta, of your third-grade class, circa 1965.

Now my oldest son is in third grade. His classroom looks much smaller than ours did, and they have partitions instead of walls. The library is now called an "LRC," and the books share space with a bank of computers. Today, they explore the broad boulevards of electronic technology, and they approach the task of reading with a "whole language" bent. It's all different, Miss Vesta, and yet it is much the same. They still have scandals at recess, oral reports, unannounced quizzes, and notes passed through chains of small, sweaty hands. And they still have report cards, of course, most of which are accompanied by the stomach-churning realities of parent-teacher conferences. My son is just beginning to understand that he should be tense about this, that there is something vaguely threatening about being formally assessed, held up to the light like a confidential letter.

I remember being tense about school, forever queasy about all those tests and measurements and hurdles that would surely expose me as something less than I was supposed to be. Anxiety always wiped my mind clean as a summer blackboard, especially on exam days, and I would come home with some mediocre score that would later spawn mediocre grades on my report card. And next to those grades were the "Comments," written in the teacher's own loopy hand, that captured her impressions of me and made the whole thing uncomfortably personal. Several of my teachers took that opportunity, Miss Vesta, to inform my parents, in case they were unaware, that I was definitely not one of those girls in starched plaid jumpers who moaned in agony when the teacher called on someone else.

Do you remember Mrs. Breen, the fifth-grade teacher? Her appraisal of me was terse: "I feel Martha is capable of doing better than average work. She rarely contributes to classroom discussion." Miss Bergren, way back in first grade, said that I did not "take initiative" or "use my time effectively." And you, Miss Vesta, probably still sitting at your desk as the sun sank low, thought about how to sum me up in a sentence or two, and finally put pen to paper. You wrote: "Martha lacks confidence in her own ability. She gives up before she tries."

I don't blame you for saying it. I'm sure it was true. I was a timid child, and I expended as little effort as possible because it seemed the safe thing to do—failing without having tried was much easier for me to swallow than extending myself and stumbling anyway. Like the tall boy who slumps in apology for his height, I kept my head low and tried not to attract attention; my fear of disapproval was much more persuasive than my urge to succeed, my need to be known.

While you were teaching science, I daydreamed that I could fly. While your chalk was clicking out math problems on the board, I was playing with sentences, writing poems, on my lined notebook paper. Words, I could manage. In their company, I felt good. I read ravenously, and looked to my books as a flower looks to the sun. It was never a part of myself I was willing to own, to wear in public like a polka-dot dress; reading and writing were my private kingdoms, sheltered places I could go, where the travails of humanity were left to the characters, and imagining their adventures, envisioning their faces, was, for me, enough.

Somehow or other, Miss Vesta, you forgave me for refusing to learn some of the lessons you were teaching. You knew I wasn't trying, you knew I could do better. Though you took note of these deficiencies, in a moment that would affect my life for years to come, you also chose to make note of my one, quiet strength. It was you who saw a calling where the others saw only obstinance and lassitude. At the close of third grade, you wrote: "I expect to be reading Martha's books and poems in a few years."

I can't say that my life would have been altered completely had you not written that sentence, but I can say that it was made more meaningful, more purposeful, in the years that followed. My parents, and my father especially, seized on your words and the future they promised; my dad believed in the mystery of God's generous hand, and he believed it was possible for a soul, my soul, to be imprinted with its own gifts, its own persistent direction. In all the gray and troubled years of my adolescence, when pimples and boyfriends came and went and I nearly failed both algebra and geometry, my father always reminded me of what you said, and he spoke of my career, my calling, as if it were a story he had seen in a thousand different dreams. He believed in me and eventually, reluctantly, I did too.

I haven't seen you for more than thirty years, Miss Vesta, and I haven't seen my father for twenty. But I remember you both, and the power of your encouragement. It is important that I remember it, especially now that I am a mother, and my son's teacher tells me that he drifts away more than he listens, that his time is seldom used effectively, that he could achieve much, much more if only he applied himself. These things he knows, and perhaps a bit too well. So it is my job to remind him that he grasps math with intuitive clarity, that he can summon facts and events from his mind that the rest of us forget, that he absorbs and loves the history of the world as if it were his own. In this mixture lies a calling, a gift, that God has left for us to find, to build upon, to form a life around.

You see, Miss Vesta, you taught me more than math and geography. You showed me, through your own example, that a few words of encouragement, a slight squeeze of the shoulder, can set in motion a carefully planned journey, a story written in God's own prose.

Thank you for your help. In a way, it was the sentence you wrote, Miss Vesta, that began this book, that began my very career, way back in the year 1965.

Love,

M

Chapter 14

Dear Christmas Spirit,

"It is easy for me to see now that magic is never summoned by self-discipline or a sleigh-full of good intentions; careful planning and Martha Stewart details do not, in and of themselves, trigger a surge of holy light."

Dear Christmas Spirit,

It was only after the Christmas tree had been dragged out to the curb and all the decorations stowed in the basement that I realized I had neither seen nor felt you during this holiday season. Certainly, there have been other years when I missed you but was too busy or preoccupied to even notice; this year, I planned for your arrival, and missed you still. You are, after all, an elusive character, a fleeting glow, whose soundless comings and goings are frequently lost, as I was, in the flashing, gift-wrapped clutter that Christmas has become. On my long list of holiday chores and obligations, there was no room left for you.

I began this season with the best of intentions. It was my theory that meticulous planning and early shopping sorties would pave the road to Christmas with spare time, spiritual focus, and a measured, deliberate tempo that would make your presence possible, even likely. I believed that greater organization would lead to less stress, and that less stress would automatically issue forth an invitation for you, Christmas Spirit, to come and be with us as the birth of Christ was celebrated.

Perhaps your invitation was misplaced in the swirl of the season, or inadvertently delivered to the Spirit of Discipline and Order; this spirit came and imbued my holiday preparations with structure and a cool sense of control. She is less personal than you, more punctual, rarely forgiving and never indulgent; she wants things done, with or without joy, with tangible sentiment or perfunctory indifference—it doesn't matter. The Spirit of Discipline and Order takes pleasure only in the task completed, the responsibility fulfilled.

There can be no question, Christmas Spirit, that my responsibilities were fulfilled. Never before have I made Christmas purchases in October, and never before have I finished them prior to Thanksgiving; I was proud of myself and probably the envy of my less diligent friends. Next, I turned my attention to the cards, all of which were signed, addressed, and stamped on schedule, during the first part of December.

I then methodically began to exhume Christmas decorations from their boxes and deck the halls of our house. The tree went up and was beautifully lit and ornamented. It was at this point that the kids' excitement began to bubble up uncontrollably in their eyes and voices; I felt their anticipation snap in the air like static electricity and, for a few moments, I let myself fly with it. But as the canyon of our vast expectations stretched wide before me, the Spirit of Anxiety wafted in and suggested, from the side of her cheerless mouth, that all the home-baked cookies and glittering ornaments and red-ribboned gifts may not be enough. Expectations this big, she hinted, can never quite be met.

You have probably discerned, Christmas Spirit, that it was not just the children's expectations that were inflated and insatiable. In the years I have been a mother, I have come to approach Christmas as an important job; it is my responsibility to see to it that my children have wondrous holidays they will remember forever. If I have failed them in any way through the year, it is at Christmas that I have an opportunity to repay those old debts and to drape my regrets with silver strands of tinsel. Wrapped up in each of my children's gifts is my runaway love for them, and my unspoken pledge to deliberately and purposefully conjure the magic of Christmas.

Writing these words in the unenchanted chill of January, Christmas Spirit, I feel like a fool. It is easy for me to see now that magic is never summoned by self-discipline or a sleigh-full of good intentions; careful planning and Martha Stewart details do not, in and of themselves, trigger a surge of holy light. Looking back, I can say that the times when I've felt your presence were always unplanned, moments when, for whatever reason, I was not doing much of anything. My mind and my hands were quiet. I was sitting in a candlelit church on Christmas Eve, or glimpsing the lights of our Christmas tree in an otherwise darkened room, or hearing a favorite carol on the radio late at night as the rest of the world slept. A feeling of awe and contentment came over me, a sense of amazement that was made singular by its effect on my soul; it was both new and familiar, temporary and unerasable, personal and infinite.

I suppose the greatest gift I can give myself and my children is a little stillness here and there, secret appointments to do nothing but appreciate the place we are in, both physically and spiritually. Maybe you will come, Christmas Spirit, and maybe you won't; you are one thing I can neither control nor organize. But we can open ourselves to the possibility of you, at Christmas and throughout the year, for I suspect that you are the same spirit who occasionally meets me in July or March or September when a moment of silent reflection inexplicably becomes meaningful and magic. Perhaps you are the Spirit of Wonder or the Spirit of Peace, mistaken all these years as one who blesses us only in December.

Come anytime, Spirit. I'll be expecting you, but only after I've learned to expect a little less of myself.

Faithfully,

M

Chapter 15

Dear Todd,

"We are brother and sister,
much closer in age than
we are in temperament,
who regard each other from
a cautious distance,
a pair of birds perched on
opposite ends of the same
power line."

Dear Todd,

It is not entirely a coincidence that I am writing you this letter just days after our most recent and senseless quarrel. The whole noisy episode made me think about the state of affairs between us, the fact that we rarely fight anymore because fighting requires a certain level of involvement, a degree of intensity between two people that is several notches higher than ours. We are brother and sister, much closer in age than we are in temperament, who regard each other from a cautious distance, a pair of birds perched on opposite ends of the same power line.

Ours is not a unique situation. While I certainly know adults who are deeply attached to their siblings, exchanging gifts and letters and affectionate memories, I know plenty of others who exchange little more than Christmas cards and the occasional cordial phone call. There is no outright adversity, no defining, prehistoric grudge that pulls at their hearts with a restless set of hands. There is love, of course, but at times it feels lifeless, tepid, like a dinner that used to be hot but was left too long on the table.

So what happened? How is it that two people who once shared a house, backseat privileges in the family sedan, an upstairs bathroom, a ratty pair of jeans, a jumble of bittersweet experience, can grow up to share only a vague resemblance and an even vaguer sense of disenchantment? Where does the drift occur, Todd? When was it that we became separated like a pair of socks in the laundry?

Looking back on our lives, I am tempted to say it was when we left for our different colleges, or when Dad died and each of us spun off into our own lonely orbits. But it was probably neither of those things. It was probably a slow, gradual movement, a subtle resentment here and a lengthy silence there, a string of small events and petty conversations that licked at our souls like an ocean's steady surf. Our expectations of one another rose and fell, rose and fell, until they finally became a fog through which we could no longer see.

It is in our expectations of one another that our problems truly grow, I suppose. From a brother or sister, we expect more than we do from our friends or our colleagues or the neighbors next door. We expect wordless understanding, compassion, the deep knowingness and acceptance that come of shared history and mutual experience. We expect, perhaps more than anything, compatibility; it stands to reason that two people raised by the same parents at the same address in the same era should be, essentially, the same. Our responses to the past should be identical, shouldn't they? So we come to our siblings looking for mirror images of ourselves and find instead relative strangers, people with views of their own, quirks that defy logic, memories that stand in stark contrast to ours, and goals and dreams that differ from our own. Maybe we just can't forgive each other for emerging from our conjoined childhoods as separate, dissimilar adults.

I'm sure you would not argue the fact that we are different from each other. According to Mom, we always have been. You are less structured in your approach to life than I am, more generous of heart and spirit, I think, though less disciplined, organized, serious than me; you are much looser than I am about most things. You are a go-with-the-flow sort of guy who ducked in and out of school, in and out of trouble, who sometimes had a job, sometimes didn't. I followed a more traditional path, staying in school, remaining continually employed since age fifteen, goal-oriented, self-sufficient, able to accomplish things with the constancy and reliability of planetary movement. It was easy for Mom and Dad to point out our many distinctions, and it was frequently clear that they preferred my way of doing things to yours. You've probably always seen me as the pampered, favored child. But what you don't know is that I always favored you, looked up to you, secretly suspected that your style was in some intangible way better than mine no matter what the grown-ups thought. There was an easiness, a freedom, about you that I wanted for myself.

It remains difficult for me to accept or even acknowledge the effect you continue to have on me. When I see you, Todd, when I hear your voice, I feel within me the rebirth of a girlhood self I prefer not to recognize. She holds you as her idol, her mentor, the other half of her own beating heart, the brother who was hers alone but who now belongs to the world. I don't want to need you, to love you so irrationally, blindly, faithfully, as I did when I was a child, but those feelings well up in me still sometimes; I resist them, I tell myself you are no superhero, no shining saint, no king who should wield such heavy influence over my adult emotions and mature sensibilities. But you do it anyway. The little-girl part of me who worshiped you loyally comes back, no questions asked, as soon as the aura of you, the very smell of you, fills up the room. I don't really want that foolish girl around anymore; perhaps I avoid you so that I can also avoid her.

But the truth is, of course, that I can avoid neither you nor her. You are both integral parts of me. There are days when it pains me that I cannot simply resign from the complexity of you, just quit all this effort like a job or a lifelong habit. I've known people who have walked out of their families, leaving behind parents and siblings and the emotional burdens they always bring with them, but it seems they never fully escape. The ones we have loved so unquestionably, so insensibly and uncontrollably, live on in our hearts with a dreadful fixedness, a permanence that outlasts the passage of time and all attempts to cleanse it out. You are indelibly imprinted on me, on my very spirit, just as I am on yours; we are to each other tattoos that cannot be removed. We are stuck with each other.

This can be no accident. God, in his infinite wisdom, could surely have arranged for us to be grouped into homogenous families where joy is spread like butter and conflicts are neatly resolved and stored in the basement. But he chose instead to pair people like you with people like me, knowing, of course, that we would not always get along. He must have had a reason. Is it possible we have in some way been instrumental in making one another strong, able to occasionally accept the unacceptable or love the unlovable, maybe even better equipped to manage the ongoing crisis that life seems to be? Yes, it is possible. It is even possible that we are like a pair of divinely made shoes, one shaped for the right foot and the other for the left, opposite yet functionally in sync, the use and beauty of one made obvious only by the existence of the other.

When I reflect on the fact that it was God who chose you to be with me, a gauzy feeling begins to cloak my senses. My frustration recedes. I find myself remembering the comfort I once took in hearing your deep-sleep breathing across the dark hall between our rooms. I remember the times you tried to protect me from boys with murky intentions. I feel again my cold grief when you were struck down by a car and no one could assure me you would live. I remember that I love you no matter what, even if I don't always want to.

You are, in ways I can't consistently understand, a gift from God, chosen specifically for me; in the process of complicating my life, you may have somehow saved it, or made it richer, or blessed it in ways I have stubbornly overlooked. Is this realization enough to spare us all future conflict, to heal all our wounds? No. But it is enough just now to make me see you in a different light, as a heavenly blessing in a brotherly disguise, and I feel hope rise up within me like the sun on a brand new day.

Love,

M

Chapter 16

Dear Green Coat,

"But you stuck with it,

chiseling and prying,

under cover of darkness,

safe in the knowledge that most

residents would be away on that

holiday weekend,

until you climbed through my

window and laid its frame across

my bed."

Dear Green Coat,

I thought of several ways I could address you in this letter—"Attacker," "Intruder," "Stalker," "Assailant"—but I settled on "Green Coat" because it is descriptive without being needlessly provocative. It is true, after all, that you wore a green nylon coat with yellow lettering on its back the night you assaulted me; while it is also true that you "attacked," "intruded," and "stalked," naming you for any of these details might put you immediately on the defensive or, worse, cause you to feel a surge of wicked power. I don't want you to feel powerful or proud as you read this. I want you to feel humble, circumspect, even a bit startled at the very thought of me. It would seem a mild form of justice, Green Coat, if today I surprised you.

Preparing to write this letter of closure has prompted me to think about you, to remember you, in much greater measure than I ordinarily would. Now that sixteen years have passed, I think of you rarely—when I find I've foolishly left a door unlocked, or I hear a noise in the night, or I come home to an empty house that feels strangely, vaguely, inhabited. These are the times when I remember your long, greasy hair, the squarish glasses you wore, the way your breath warmed the back of my neck as you gripped me from behind. I remember the entire scene in the patchy way one remembers a dream. But the terror and confusion that roiled through my mind always come back to me vivid as a murderous urge, jagged as a broken window.

Sometimes, Green Coat, I wonder what you were thinking and feeling as you used your knife to chip away at my window frame until it came loose in your hands. There were security bars on that window too which must have tested your patience and criminal resolve. But you stuck with it, chiseling and prying, under cover of darkness, safe in the knowledge that most residents would be away on that holiday weekend, until you climbed through my window and laid its frame across my bed. You were in. You were in my home.

What did you do first? Maybe you went through my desk right away since it was near the window; from one of its drawers you took a sheet of first-class stamps. From my dresser you removed a pair of inexpensive earrings and an opal necklace that was given to me by a friend. There was some change for the bus too that you shoveled into your pockets. It was not much of a haul, even for a small-time, inexperienced thief like you. But then, you knew there wouldn't be much worth taking in a basement-level studio apartment that was modest by any standard. You could see from outside that there was nothing of value there.

Maybe for that reason, along with a few others, the police concluded that it was not really money or goods that you came looking for. It was their theory that you knew me, that you knew I lived in that specific apartment and had probably observed me there from a place nearby. They suspected that you lived in a neighboring building, saw me from your window or out on the street, and made it your peculiar business to find a way into my home and into my life.

You did indeed become an irrevocable part of my life when you made the decision to wait for me after filching a thing or two, to crouch behind my door instead of fleeing back out the window you originally entered. I remember you had the lights off; when I walked in at midnight with my very intoxicated friend, Sandy, the first thing I did was switch on the lamp. I turned around to close the door and there you were, knife extended, standing between me and the apartment's only exit.

Sandy had flopped down on the floor and was close to passing out—I'm sure you were surprised by her arrival, just as I was surprised by yours. I asked you what you wanted. I offered you money. As I reached for my purse, you circled around behind me and pressed your knife to my neck; all the while I was shouting at you, shouting for Sandy to get up and help me, shouting in the vain hope that a neighbor might hear me.

I remember Sandy, still sprawled across the floor, lifting her head from the carpet to say, "Martha, do you know this guy?" Green Coat, I think it was after one of her questions that you said, "Sandy, stay on the floor." Digging the knife a bit deeper into my skin, you said, "You get on the bed."

I think it was the idea of being on a bed with you, the idea of being raped, that caused me to fill up with wrath and strength and a feeling of utter clarity. God must have made me aware of your slightly hesitant approach to this ugly incursion, he must have shaken Sandy awake and enabled her to think, because all at once, everything changed. I pulled your knife off my neck and ordered you out of my home. Angry at this change in the weather, exasperated by my uncooperative mood, you shut off the lamp, thinking perhaps that darkness would empower you in the way that Popeye is empowered by spinach. I turned the lamp back on, and we struggled as it fell to the floor. The next thing I recall was seeing Sandy, furious and suddenly sober, standing in front of the door she had miraculously managed to open. She pushed you out into the hall as you stabbed at her stomach with your knife. There was more shouting, and then, by God's grace, you were gone, running down the hall like a wounded, defeated dog. I never saw you again.

I won't bore you with the details of the cynical, halfhearted police investigation, the reactions of my family and friends, the cold draft that blew through my soul every time I came home to that apartment in the following weeks. As you probably noticed, I moved out within a month or so, thinking I could escape my memories and the dreadful smell of invasion.

It would be easy for me to say that your assault on me that night scarred me for life. I could tell you how nervous I've been, how cautious and suspicious, how permanently engrossed in the arts of self-defense and home security. As much as I want you to feel remorseful about that night, and as much as I want to blame you for all my problems and fears, I would be lying if I said you had ruined me. I would be giving you credit for a job not done.

Actually, Green Coat, you changed me, and the course of my life, in ways that were perhaps meant to be. Had you not attacked me in 1980, I might not have been as watchful or ready in future crime scenarios (you were neither the first nor the last to threaten or rob me, but you were the only one who came into my house to do it). I would not have moved to my sunny, second-floor apartment, where I forged some close friendships and entered a happier stage of life. Because I had a roommate and a lower share of rent to pay, I took a risk and quit an unrewarding job to begin writing in earnest. The years that followed were some of my most productive and enjoyable. All of these good things came to pass because of you, Green Coat, or, more accurately, because you compelled me to move forward, to act radically and decisively, in a life that was slightly stagnant and none-too-fulfilling.

So, while I am certainly not grateful to you or overwhelmed with feelings of sweet forgiveness, I am at peace with the whole thing. Standing high on the hill of hindsight, I think I can safely say that only by losing some property and a bit of equilibrium did I gain the momentum to do something different, something that now seems like part of a larger plan; the great irony may be, Green Coat, that I took away much more from our moments together than you managed to take away from me.

From behind locked doors,

M

Chapter 17

Dear Grandpa,

"Mom and I fret about money,
we fret about everything,
because we simply don't believe
we will emerge from
life's complexities intact."

Dear Grandpa,

Hi. It's me—Martha. I trust the connection between heaven and earth is clear today and that you will receive these thoughts and feel the strength of my yearning for the days when you were here. I miss you, Grandpa. I miss the clack-clack sound of your old typewriter. I miss your Ivory soap smell and the soft hiss of your breathing as you slept in your chair. I wish we could talk as we used to, quietly, without pretense or flair, about whatever it was that came to mind. Instead, I will talk to you here, on this page, and know that you are somewhere near, listening.

I could think of no one better to come to than you with my nagging concerns about money. Does that surprise you? I imagine it might. You were never a financial wizard or a wheeler-dealer of any sort. I think it would be safe to say, Grandpa, that money was no more important to you than the condition of your shoelaces or the political improprieties of nations overseas. You always seemed to possess a casual disregard for money and the things it could buy; somewhere along the line, you set aside the issues of finance and ambition as an old woman sets aside her knitting at the end of the day. Was it just a simpler time when you grew up, or were you endowed with a confidence, an assurance in both yourself and the world, that blanketed your worries and lulled them to sleep? It mystifies me, Grandpa, that some people are so nonchalant about money, while others, like me, allow it to have so much power.

It's not that we are in any kind of financial trouble. Everything is fine on that front; our investments are sound, our papers in order. But still, despite our relative security, I fret about money obsessively, endlessly, like a mother wrings her hands over a child out past curfew. There is a persistent anxiety in my heart, a penetrating sense of dread, that something could go wrong, our lives could change forever, if our bank accounts are not fat enough to sustain us. I cringe over minor expenses and unforeseen fees as if they will unravel this tidy life of mine in a single, ghastly moment.

How did I get this way? I have never known real financial deprivation. Not once have I had to go without a meal or patch holes in my shoes or walk a long, icy distance to look for work. I have always had enough, and most of the time plenty, but the fear of not having enough lingers in my consciousness like the odor of last night's dinner.

I suppose I could blame Mom and Dad who, for me, re-presented the yin and yang of spending attitudes. Dad worked hard and periodically liked to blow some money; without warning and definitely without permission, he would come home with a new TV or a desk the size of Montana. Then Mom, predictable as the change of seasons, would throw a fit and loudly maintain that, because of this unplanned and extravagant purchase, we were headed for certain destitution. I suppose it would make sense, from a pop-psychological perspective, for me to simply assume the role of whistle blower in my own family, and perhaps I have. But, more importantly, I think I have inherited my mother's lack of faith, the bleak, Lord-help-us outlook that underlies anxiety. Mom and I fret about money, we fret about everything, because we simply don't believe we will emerge from life's complexities intact.

Mom's penchant for worry probably traces back to the 1930s. When you lost your job in the Depression, Grandpa, and had to sell your house and move in with your in-laws (with whom you lived for many, many years), Mom was young; those losses left a deep and lasting impression on her, just as a serious wound will leave a flat, pearly scar. Whatever confidence she may have had in a safe, reliable world slipped out of her soul like steam from a kettle. Now she hordes things—canned goods, old appliances, craft supplies from the 1960s—just in case. Her many possessions form a moat between herself and pending disaster; my savings account performs the same task for me.

Like Mom, I learned at an early age that things can go awry, suddenly and flamboyantly, and learned too that it is always best to assume the very worst, to put faith in nothing but the inevitable disappointments just around the bend. Lending strength to my concern about money is a deeper and more troubling commitment to protecting myself against potential calamity. The ups and downs of life with alcoholic parents left me off-balance, I guess, and taught me that a perfectly ordinary day can suddenly turn black, or spin like a top, or dish out human failure in large, sloppy doses. It was very early in life that I learned to protect myself against unexpected reversals by constantly expecting them, by preparing for them as I would for a hurricane or an audit with the IRS. Somehow, it made me feel safer, more ready, if I envisioned disaster before it arrived. Still, I was always taken aback by the outrageous dramas that played out in my home; no matter how well I prepared, there was pain and fear and an awful sense of chaos.

It seems obvious to me now that my worries about money are merely a symptom, a superficial expression, of the same hopelessness and panoramic distrust that continues to plague my mother. Perhaps it is those childhood experiences of loss or unpredictability that make some of us fretful and insecure, while others, like you, Grandpa, coast through life with bundles of positive assumptions and favorable perspectives tied to the tops of your cars. It's not that you never worried—I'm sure you did—but your faith in the world's essential goodness and in your own ability to persevere were always bigger than the troubles that passed through your days.

Now that I've identified the ailment, I must set about curing it, right? If only it were that easy. It is a job of unbelievable scope, this changing of outlook and attitude. I am so thankful that I don't have to do it alone. Perhaps you've heard, Grandpa, that I've been actively searching for spiritual depth which, though joyful, has brought my worries to center stage. I'm finding that faith cannot exist in a vacuum; it must be accompanied by hope, an abiding belief that God will answer prayers and act in our best interest, and a willingness to leave the issues of my life in God's very capable hands. Once I ask him for help, I am free to go without the bulky burden of anxiety; nevertheless, I drag it with me still. Despite its erosion of my spirit, worry has become something of a friend to me, a companion that walks around with me in darkness and light and keeps me from seeing things clearly. It warns against trust, in both God and the people around me, and it encourages the sort of watchfulness that casts long shadows across my view of the world.

It appears, Grandpa, that I must give up this old friend in order to make room for the joy and hope that God brings with him. Hope cannot live alongside fear, trust cannot bloom in the company of worry. I wish you were here to reassure me as you once did, but I will have to rely on faith instead, on God's great patience, to keep me moving along this steep though rewarding path. If you see me pause, Grandpa, to count my money or worry about the future, come see me in my dreams, as you often have, comfortably ensconced in your chair, asleep in the midst of the world's pandemonium, the very image of trust and hope and quiet, blessed assurance.

Love,

M

Chapter 18

Dear God,

"You see, God, though I want to
change spiritually,
in matters of the soul and heart,
I am afraid of mutating
to such a pronounced degree
that I will alienate
my family and friends."

Dear God,

I've been waiting for you to make a real Christian of me, Father, and you have been waiting for me too. Of course, you are more patient than me. You are so patient, in fact, that you have awaited my wholehearted devotion to you for all the years of my life, all the years in which I've come within your reach and then stepped back again, dancing my dance of ambivalence in outdated shoes.

It's not that I don't believe in you, God. And it's not that I can't understand your teachings. I think the problem lies in my private expectations; I carry within me a set of assumptions about the way it should feel to be a believer, the way it should look and sound and behave on the stage of human existence. I have a certain idea of what a Christian is, and it is not like me. So I have been waiting for a metamorphosis. I have been waiting to become an authentic member of the Christian throng.

My first exposure to Christianity in bloom was through my father. I'm sure I had known believers before, but never had I seen someone travel from a state of benign acknowledgment of you to a condition of feverish dedication. From my twelve- or thirteen-year-old vantage point, it appeared that my dad had been changed in the sweeping way that the earth is changed by its seasons. There was nothing halfway or equivocal about his transformation, nothing subtle or understated. With a blare of trumpets and a scattering of rose petals, my father's entry into the realm of belief was made known to the world.

Suddenly, we were stalwart churchgoers. Religious magazines began to accumulate in our house and in the houses of all our friends to whom my father sent gift subscriptions. He began reading to us from inspirational books, and he charitably read them every Saturday afternoon to a ragtag group of seniors at a local nursing home. Local missionaries were invited into our home to school us on the Bible, which my father quoted from liberally. Not a day went by when Dad did not find some biblical text to back up an idea he was fond of. ("Honor thy mother and father" was a special favorite of his.)

As a child, I could not yet fathom the depth of my father's inner growth, the breadth of his inner joy; I did not understand his conversion as the meaningful, uplifting thing it surely was for him. Instead, I focused in my youth on the external trappings of faith, on the visible changes and abrupt upheaval in the rhythm of our house. I was confused, even a little scared. What I thought I had known about my dad became obsolete, and I wasn't sure how I felt about the new man who was now wearing my father's clothes. He seemed different, and he wanted me to be different too. I think I might have been happier for him in his newfound faith if he had not tried so strenuously to take me with him; I didn't really want to go anywhere, I didn't want to change or leave the naive, irresponsible haven of childhood too soon. I just wanted to continue being me.

It was just a few years after Dad died that I witnessed yet another rebirth. Katherine, a woman who worked for the same company I did, needed a roommate just as I began to search for one. She was even younger than I was, and at a point in her life when she felt an acute need for direction. Shortly after we moved in together, she found what she was looking for in you, Lord; she joined a church, her brother's church, and proceeded to alter her life, her interests, her thinking, in the same radical way that a caterpillar approaches the task of becoming a butterfly. The woman I was just beginning to know seemed to become someone else.

Once again, I was caught in the eddy of another's transformation. Katherine, like my father, came to know you in a rapid, dramatic fashion; there could be no conversation with her, no matter how mundane or blandly informational, that did not include your name. She dropped all her old friends and associated solely with members of her church. She even changed her diet to conform to her burgeoning sense of spiritual health—she seemed to regard me with barely camouflaged disapproval whenever I heedlessly drank a cup of coffee. Soon enough, Katherine surprised me with the news that she would be quitting her job, moving out of our apartment, and going to live out west where she would attend a church-affiliated college. Her metamorphosis was complete, and she vanished from my life like a pencil mark erased.

In my mind are etched these "before" and "after" snapshots. I have known plenty of other Christians, but they were among the faithful when I met them so I never saw them "before." I could only assume they were different than they once had been, that they had waved good-bye to their former selves when they set sail on the ship of Christianity.

I have been waiting on the pier for the past year or so, ready to cruise but not sure I have a valid passport. I've been waiting for the change in me that would signal the onset of true Christianity, expecting it and, at the same time, dreading it. You see, God, though I want to change spiritually, in matters of the soul and heart, I am afraid of mutating to such a pronounced degree that I will alienate my family and friends; I don't want to turn my life upside-down or to become one of those aggressive, in-your-face Christians who thrust their righteousness at every passerby. It is not my style to grind out biblical quotations like pepper from a mill, and I love my friends too much to leave them behind. I don't want to become my father or Katherine. I just want to become a more patient and forgiving version of the person you created me to be.

As I have worked these past few days to compose this letter, you have shown me two things, God. One of them is this: my father and Katherine did not change as much as I tend to believe they did. Both of them were exuberant, zealous individuals before their religious conversions; Dad's style was never tepid or apologetic, and he shared his notions on politics and world affairs just as generously and emphatically as he advertised his faith. Katherine, like Dad, was neither shy nor wishy-washy about much of anything; before you came into her life, God, she talked about boyfriends and clothes and the other stars in her galaxy with the same enthusiasm and passion she brought to her newfound belief. You did not resculpt her, God. Katherine, like Dad, painted her Christianity with the broad, flamboyant brush of her own personality.

The other insight you have given me, God, is that I have already been changed by my experience of you. There are external differences—I have been moved to go to church, to participate in ministries, to write a book with a spiritual emphasis—and there are subterranean differences in the way I think and feel. My soul has been gradually refurbished like an old house; it is the same house, yet it is made better, stronger, with some new beams and supports and a warmer furnace at its core.

Thank you, God, for your subtle architecture and appreciation of the existing structure. I am still me, introspective at times and impatient at others, quietly faithful, ever seeking an end to my fears, and now, perhaps, able to understand that the expression of my faith is as unique as the house in which it lives.

With great love,

M

Chapter 19

Dear Matthew and Kevin,

"But more than any of its
puzzles could imply,
the state of motherhood
is a state of profound
and moving love;
it is as simple,
and as complicated, as that."

Dear Matthew
and Kevin,

I 'll write you this letter today, but give it to you on some far-away tomorrow. With these words, I'll try to explain what it means to me to be your mother, and it's really not the sort of thing six- and eight-year-old boys understand. In fact, it's not even something I consistently understand; when I try to wrap my arms around the secrets of motherhood, to plumb their ambiguities and decipher their codes, they wriggle free and run just ahead of me, like the horizon, in my sight but ever distant, never possessed.

To be a parent is to be a walker of lines; the boundary between good and not-so-good mothering is translucent, shifty, different for one than it is for another. I am continually trying to fathom how to love but not smother you, how to guide but not control you, how to discipline but not bind you. I worry that my ministrations will somehow fall short of your needs; I worry too that if I accommodate your needs too well, you will become men who accommodate others not at all. In our cause-and-effect universe, I wonder what cause of mine will become an effect of yours.

My self-consciousness is showing now, like a lacy slip from beneath my dress. Perhaps it is simply the nasty tangle of perfectionism that makes me so tentative, so uncertain, in this mother role. I know from experience how the problems of parents permeate a household, how they inevitably come to rest on the thin, rounded shoulders of the children, who then carry them, like heavy sacks of coal, as if they were their own. I remember how it felt to live with troubled, preoccupied adults who had so little left for me; as a child, I always promised myself I would be a different kind of parent, better, patient, more involved. In my youth, I dreamed of a way to do it perfectly.

But, of course, it was only a dream. There is no ideal in the spectrum of parenthood. Determined not to repeat the mistakes of my parents, I have made plenty of my own. At times I ask too much of you, at others not enough. I am forever torn between the joys of indulging and pleasing you, and the responsibilities of teaching and governing you. You need both softness and strength from me, freedom and structure. I want to give it all to you, in just the right amounts and at just the right time, but the subtleties of that recipe elude me like algebraic solutions.

It took me a while to fully appreciate the fact that I am not one parent but two; you boys are very different from one another, and you each need your own kind of mother. You, Matthew, are the cerebral one, the boy who thinks incessantly and talks just as much, who relies on his intellect to process the marvels of the world, and who drinks in knowledge like sand soaks up rain. You are a lover of routines, a boy who feasts on the measurement of things, the sanity, the safety, of numbers; I think it is true, Matthew, that you prefer the clean sphere of known quantities to the unruly kingdom of emotions.

From me, you need many things. You rely on me as a fact-checker, as both a source of ideas and an echo chamber for your own. You count on me to loosen the twine of your serious nature and, when you are occasionally overtaken by a rush of deep-down feelings, you bring them to me in a disheveled bundle; together, we look at them, we sort and smooth them as we would a heap of fresh laundry, until your heart beats comfortably again.

Kevin, you are a child of another variety. Your life is a series of impulses, a stream of unpasteurized emotion. Although your mind is a busy, productive place, it is your heart that holds the keys to your character. You are a child who loves openly and without apology, a boy whose feelings are embroidered across the front of his shirt. Even though you love to stage violent crashes with your Matchbox cars, you cannot watch the movie *Hook* because of a single scene wherein a baby is sorrowfully separated from its mother. It has been a year since you've seen it, but the memory of that scene makes your eyes fill with tears.

As a sensitive boy, Kevin, you need my reassurance. You need to know that you are loved, secure, in a safe place that is yours for all time. The idea of change, of impermanence, makes you feel afraid; it upsets you when I get new glasses or change my hair, and you need for me to tell you that everything is okay, nothing important has been tampered with, our lives will continue without interruption. You need plenty of affection and regular reminders that your efforts are worthwhile. It is essential for you to feel included. I do my best to keep the garden of you well tended.

At times I feel more equipped to navigate the personality of one of you than the other; there are days when the needs of one will overwhelm, while the other offers solace. You see, boys, as we negotiate the finer points of your life stories, I find I am re-negotiating my own in the process. It is not always pleasant. Your fresh, unfiltered emotions, Kevin, evoke waves of feeling in me—the pain of your childhood hurts throb at the back of my throat, because they were once my hurts too. Matthew, your intellect cushions and disguises your heart, but I see it anyway, I know its contours, because it is a newer, less life-worn version of mine. Parts of me appear in parts of you, boys, and I fight the urge to fix or suppress them; it is important that the vivid colors of you be uncompromised, undiluted, by my dissatisfaction with me.

But, more than any of its puzzles could imply, the state of motherhood is a state of profound and moving love; it is as simple, and as complicated, as that. Your presence on this planet is a blessing, an opening-up of love and sheer, wonderful possibility, that I have yet to recover from. I look at you and I see miracles. You are gifts to me from God himself; when I am lifted up and made weak in the knees by the sight of your sleeping faces, or by the sound of your pouring-out laughter, I feel the reality of God like a breeze on my face. It is a privilege to know this depth of love, to be child of God and mother of you all in one sweeping moment.

And, my sons, it is a privilege to be filled up by the two of you, to be so frankly smitten, to learn the music of your chiming souls, to be a beam that lights your way as you grow up, as I grow, slowly, gratefully, with you.

Love,

Mom

Chapter 20

Dear Fat,

"Until I was ready to unravel
my emotional mysteries and face
myself more honestly,
I put considerable energy into
sustaining you, my protector, my
least demanding friend."

Dear Fat,

It's been a while since you and I have been together; what used to be an intense, needed relationship between us has withered to an indifferent acquaintance, a nod of recognition as we pass on the street. I remember you as I would an old boyfriend, with a modest, grudging form of fondness, a smattering of sentiment, and a much larger dose of hallelujah-good-riddance freedom. The truth is, Fat, I'm glad you are gone from me and, at the same time, I'm a little grateful you once served as my silent, faithful friend.

My earliest experience with you was in third grade, when I was eight. My brother had been hit by a car and was hospitalized in serious condition for three weeks. It was an extremely anxious time for our family, and my parents kept a vigil at Todd's bedside from morning till night. I was sent to stay with my grandparents, whom I loved with all of my being, but whose gentle gestures were not quite enough to compensate for the loss, however temporary, of my home, my family, the consoling smell of our daily, taken-for-granted lives.

There was a hole inside me I needed to fill, so I began to eat. You know how grandmothers are, Fat. They love to feed children and, as my grandmother suffered acute despair over Todd's condition, she took to feeding me as her own source of solace. Food became a conversation between us, an agreement, a balm which we could smooth over each other's aches and worries. In the space of a week or so, Fat, you came to join us, resting on my midsection in your vaguely fluid style.

I may never forget the day my mother first noticed your arrival. Perhaps you were bulging out from beneath my shirt or pushing too hard against the boundaries of my pants. She looked at me, but what she saw was you. "Mother!" she said to my grandma. "What have you done to her?" She was horrified and, for a moment, so was I. But I must have realized in some basement-level compartment of my soul that I had my mother's attention, I had stolen it back from the still-hospitalized Todd, and this sweet gift had been restored to me all because of you.

For the next few years, Fat, you helped me in your own distinct way; your presence garnered my mother's ongoing concern and preoccupation, and kept her engaged in the day-to-day fluctuations of my childhood diet. It was her goal to get rid of you by holding my weight steady as nature added an inch or two to my height. Eventually, her plan succeeded, and you were just a memory, an unfortunate circumstance that had cushioned me, ever so slightly, against the many other unfortunate circumstances of the grade-school years.

When the rigors of adolescence set in, Fat, you again assumed an important position in my life. This time, though, you were my nemesis, an enemy to be avoided at all costs, as thinness became a coveted prize to which all of us girls aspired. I had to sacrifice all traces of your fleshy comforts, even if it meant skipping both breakfast and lunch, and eating so many carrot sticks my fingers turned yellow. You were a symbol of weakness, and as I reached for independence and the right to run my own life, it seemed fitting that my body pay bony homage to my inner quest for control.

It was my devotion to control that kept me from ever surrendering to you completely, but I came as close as I dared to doing so in college. Perhaps it was the separation from home and family, a loss felt just as sharply at eighteen as it was at eight, that prompted me to eat with abandon and, subconsciously, to once again make a bid for my mother's attention. This time, all it got me was a plump posterior, new jeans large enough to enclose it, and a dogged sense that I was inferior, undisciplined, and plainly unacceptable to myself and others.

But, Fat, as miserable as I was in your company, you became my greatest, truest ally. Acting as both buffer and excuse, you enabled me to blame something other than myself (namely, you) for my romantic disappointments and social inadequacies. Whenever I felt anger or pain rising up within me like a rain-swollen river, I would sneak into the kitchen and gorge myself on spoonfuls of peanut butter, slabs of spongy cake, thick squares of brownie. The food pushed my feelings back down and anesthetized the pain; the flab that resulted was both my reward and my punishment, my armor and my shame.

As long as I had you in my life, Fat, there was room for little else. I thought about you when I woke up in the morning, when I pulled on the day's too-snug outfit, when I sat down to a meal or quietly measured my worth against the trim silhouette of another woman's waist. You consumed me, and that's the way I needed it to be. Without the distraction of you, Fat, I would have had time to see my uncertain future, my heart full of longing, my godless pursuit of the world's cheapest offerings. I was too busy with you, too obsessed to pay much attention to feelings and fears, hopes and desires. I wasn't ready to deal with those difficult, relentless suitors, so I clung to your familiar mass instead.

Though thin people tend to think of you, Fat, as a by-product of indulgent eating and unchecked laziness, you are actually made possible by the hard work of avoidance and the effortful search for compensation. For me, the extra pounds were merely the outward symptom of a concerted, rigorous drive to deny anger, to shut out pain. Until I was ready to unravel my emotional mysteries and face myself more honestly, I put considerable energy into sustaining you, my protector, my least demanding friend.

It amazes me that I ever managed to let go of you. That too is hard work. After dozens of diets and years of self-recrimination, I finally delved into my psyche to locate your stronghold. There was a lot of therapy involved, a lot of feeling, raw and uncontrollable, and I learned, quite slowly, to tolerate the up-and-down wanderings of emotion. Once I stopped trying to suppress my feelings, I made peace with them. Only then could I begin the task of saying good-bye to you.

I met my future husband, who gave me the love and attention I had so long been seeking, just as the ties between you and me were coming undone. Not too long after, I gave birth to my children, and my love for them filled up the empty spaces once occupied by you. Suddenly, there was not enough time for you, not enough room, and without my even realizing it, you slipped out of my life like an outgrown lover. You had been replaced.

But I think it is important, Fat, to point out that you were not replaced by my husband or my sons. Instead, you were supplanted by me, the essential parts of my nature I had tried to corral like unpredictable horses. All those years, I failed to see that being myself, all of myself, was enough, that I had the resources I needed in the myriad and perplexing corridors of my own God-given spirit. Fat, you were not a burden that someone else could lift from me; rather, I had to choose to know my own heart, in both its happiness and its suffering, and I had to choose to give up the seductive diversion, the enveloping hideaway, of you.

No longer yours,

M

Chapter 21

Dear Mom,

"Not once did it occur to me
that my expectations
of you were unreasonable,
a fantasy,
and that revising them
would be much more sensible
than waiting for you to
meet them."

Dear Mom,

In the years that I've been writing, there have been no essays or letters devoted to the topic of you. Dad, on the other hand, has been a pet subject of mine, cropping up in all sorts of stories like a mythic figure in a recurring dream. I think it's a little easier for me to write about Dad, mostly because he's been gone such a long time. My years with Dad are over; they've been tagged and filed, analyzed and categorized, put away in a box marked "chapters—finished." Unlike you, Dad is not living in a town nearby, adding new scenes to a drama that is already thickly plotted.

Ours is not a particularly combustible relationship, but neither is it a simple one. We are, after all, mother and daughter.

There are certain tensions that come with that territory, just as waves are a part of the sea. We pull each other close, then push each other away, saying one moment "I need you," and the next, "Get out of my way."

Maybe it's a natural parent-child rhythm, a way that generations dance with each other in the ongoing tussle of "family." But I think the pattern of our relationship is more like a race than it is like a tango, more focused upon pace and position than it is upon music and harmony. Though we are each other's advocates, we are each other's adversaries too.

Did I ever tell you about the first time Dad caught me with cigarettes? I must have been about fourteen. He called me to his desk and showed me the Marlboros he'd discovered in my room. He paid me the fifty cents they were worth in 1972, and solemnly advised me about the dangers of smoking. Though he was a smoker himself, it was your sooty lungs and habitual cough he relied upon to illustrate tobacco's eventual toll. "You don't want to cough like your mother," he said. "You don't want to be like your mother."

While he had not always been so explicit, Dad often made it clear that it was not your example I should follow. He was worried that I would learn from you and become a thorn in the side of the man I would someday marry. You were, in his estimation, full of ideas and attitudes unbecoming to a woman, a wife—he felt you were argumentative, rebellious, self-indulgent, and not at all interested in fulfilling your domestic duties. He railed against your habits daily, and I heard every word. The lesson I learned was plain: to gain Dad's approval and stay out of trouble, I needed to be compliant, cooperative, as different from you as day is from night.

Looking back, Mom, I wonder if you saw it all as a kind of betrayal. Instead of ignoring Dad's high expectations and resisting his influence as you did, I chose compliance and unwittingly became his ally, his apprentice. The spotlight on your insurgent nature was made brighter, hotter, by my obedience. You might have believed that I was making you look bad, that the red streak in your personality looked too bold against the paler backdrop of me. Dad complimented me and chastised you. The stage was set for jealousy and adolescent rivalry. Like sisters, we jockeyed for position. And thus was born the competitive undercurrent that would run like a river between us for many years to come.

It's not that we've ever been at war, per se, although there have been some nasty conflicts along the way. The on-and-off friction between you and me has typically been more subtle than outright argument, a matter of buried resentment rather than bald hostility. We've always been prone to criticizing and undermining one another. Instead of celebrating each other's successes, we tend to question them, quietly insinuating that there might be something faulty about the other's source of happiness. It is as if a victory for one spells failure for the other. It seems to me, Mom, that in our respective efforts to feel good about ourselves, it somehow became necessary for each of us to feel superior to the other, to feel that we had won. We let our ancient insecurities push love to the side.

We've never talked about this, Mom, and I feel both shame and relief as I put it on paper. Here we are, mother and daughter, still partially swept up in the petty race of siblings even now, twenty years after Dad's death. It would be fair to say that I've often wanted you to be a less difficult kind of mother, one who bakes homespun advice into her oatmeal cookies, one who wears cozy little cardigans and plays bridge on Tuesday. Perhaps it was Harriet Nelson or June Cleaver I was looking for just behind your eyes, just beneath your skin. I wanted you to be mild instead of spicy, supportive and not competitive. But in all these years, I have not succeeded in changing you. So now it is time to change myself.

I've never noticed it before, Mom, but clenched in my hand is Dad's old measuring stick. You never quite succeeded in meeting my lofty maternal ideals, just as you never quite succeeded in fulfilling Dad's expectations for a perfect wife. Dad and I each pushed you to be someone else and, when you went on being who you are, we let our disappointment become far too big and far too important.

I'm sorry, Mom, for having learned some early childhood lessons a bit too well, and for having learned some others not at all. I never considered the idea that accepting you would be far easier than trying to change you. Not once did it occur to me that my expectations of you were unreasonable, a fantasy, and that revising them would be much more sensible than waiting for you to meet them. Frequently, Mom, I get caught up in the dream world of what *should* be, rather than spending my days in the real and mostly imperfect realm of what *is*.

Maybe now we can begin the hard work of knowing each other as mother and daughter, with no agenda beyond love itself. I hope you can meet me halfway, Mom, and that you'll see my hands extended out toward you, open, ready to take hold of yours so we can run along the rest of life's route together, as a genuine team, as a circle of love unto each other, unto ourselves.

Love always,

M

Chapter 22

Dear Grandma,

"Perhaps old age is nothing
but a sifting process,
a cleaning out of drawers
and closets to find the few
great things worth
holding on to."

Dear Grandma,

I've been dreaming lately about aging. As part of the process, I suppose, I dream of you, think of you, because you are the only woman I watched grow from old to aged. You were always old to me, and it never occurred to my child-mind that you were growing up along with me, adding years slowly and carefully, like a windowsill collects dust and tiny gadgets. You did it well, without complaint. I like to think of you and your oldness.

Here is what I dream of: I am old and not at all displeased about it. I live in a small seaside cottage somewhere along the Atlantic coast. I have a wonderful garden in which I putter every morning, tending and fussing because it makes me feel needed.

There is a slight roundness to my physique, and I don't care. I have an old bike in the garage that I ride to the store sometimes, and a cat who dotes on me in a detached, cat-like way. There are several hundred books in my house and I have read them all. Some of them are my own work, collections of essays and perhaps a novel or two, and I write every day about the thoughts that continue to circle through my mind. My life is like a balmy summer evening.

These are perhaps the naive thoughts of a person who has never been old or the rantings of a harried woman who craves a little solitude. You might read them and conclude that I have much to learn between now and my seventieth birthday and that is precisely why I am writing to you. I want to learn, I want to prepare. I don't want to arrive at old age and be surprised by it, outraged at its numerous indignities and bold, unreasonable demands. If I can grow old with my eyes open, having accepted that I will indeed become aged and change in both body and mind, then perhaps I can be at peace with the whole thing and not mad as a hornet. It seems to me that so many old people are cranky because they've gotten frail and slow and tottery and they never really thought it would happen to them. It's as if you just wake up one day and suddenly find you can no longer bend down to tie your shoe.

I tend to imagine that my body will be transformed but my mind will not. I assume that my interests will be the same as they are now, and my ambitions too. But it occurs to me that I may be underestimating the effect of the body on the mind. It could be that an aching hip or a cluster of cataracts will throw water on the flame of my existence. I may no longer care very much about the content of my days. It could, with no fanfare or grand announcement, become simpler to stay in bed through most of the morning than to rise and make my way across the room and find my toothbrush or my slippers or a book that's disappeared. If it takes me two hours and a great deal of pain and planning to take a bath, I may just skip it.

In my dreams, of course, I do not smell of urine or sweat or yesterday's lunch. There are no coffee dribblings on the front of my dress. People continue to find me interesting and marvel at my wit and lively mind. There are no patronizing smiles or over-loud responses, and my youngish neighbors do not exchange glances when I tell a story they have heard from me just the day before. If other drivers are irritated with my slow, methodical ways, I have not noticed. Telephone solicitors don't fool me for a minute.

It is frightening to think of old age in the realm of its many real possibilities. Maybe it's silly of me to think that I can pre-pare for it. What I am really doing, I suppose, is trying to intel-lectualize it—if I can study it and run my hands over its crag-gy, uneven surface, hold it up to the light and know it inti-mately, then perhaps it will become something that I can con-trol. Even as my body mounts its ultimate mutiny against me, I can believe that I'm a part of that great movement, rather than its target, if I am in on the plan. It will feel more like a choice than an order.

When I was a child and thought you were old, you were barely past middle age. Your hair was deceptively white beneath those jaunty little caps you always wore. The yellow car you drove was frequently seen about town; you were busy with bridge clubs and a part-time job and the subtle ministrations of a long, faithful marriage and a dozen endless friendships. You were outgoing and opinionated, and the clerks at Steben's grocery all knew you by name. Your bedroom smelled of lilies of the valley. There was always a brooch on the bosom of your dress.

And then, ever so slowly, you began to misplace the small particulars of your life. The names for things—vase, brassiere, hatpin—began to elude you. You'd reach for them, searching through your memory just as you might fumble through your purse, and come up empty. "Whoever would have thought I would lose my mind?" you asked. Not me. I never really thought you would lose your mind, but somehow you did.

Do you remember? Probably not. It was a long, slow descent. You carried on, and so did we. But then you failed your driver's test, quit your job because counting change was too hard, mistakenly thought you'd eaten dinner when all you'd really had was an olive. Grandpa said that you tried to hit him, believing him to be a stranger who stubbornly refused to leave your house. During the night, you would get up and roam around, muttering something about a party downstairs or a pressing engagement at an unknown place. You seemed so sure, but it was four in the morning.

You stopped responding to "Grandma" or "Mom," so we all called you by your first name. Once you became Henrietta to me, it made it easier to separate the woman you had been from the child you were becoming. It was then that I began to grieve for my lost grandmother. It was then that I came to love Henrietta, the girl who now lived in my grandmother's body.

Henrietta was preoccupied with the comings and goings of a long-ago life. Her mother was back from the dead. Unnamed men paid Henrietta much attention, and she had interesting places to go. There was a sweet, dreamy smile on her face some-times, and she enjoyed lively conversations with household objects and plain, thin air.

Of course, she had no idea who I was. When I cut her hair, she assumed I was her hairdresser. It didn't matter. I never cared what she called me, so overwhelmed was I by her absolute joy in seeing me. Henrietta loved me, with no history, no blood connection, no reason why. The petty details and circumstances of my identity were of no consequence in the hours I spent with Henrietta.

Maybe the love was something you left behind, like a plant or a set of linens, for the new tenant to find. Or maybe the essential you was there all along, Grandma, living with Henrietta, loaning her the few things she really needed—summertime dresses and practical shoes, an independent nature and hardheaded vigor and a pure, unceasing will to love.

I feel a little bit heartened. Perhaps old age is nothing but a sifting process, a cleaning out of drawers and closets to find the few great things worth holding on to. What seems too precious to lose today may be tomorrow's good-riddance. The priorities of life may shift, leaving us with vision instead of sight, inner freedom in place of outer restraint.

Vigor was a fleeting privilege for your body, Grandma, but the eternal fiber of your spirit. Love might have been forgotten by your mind but it was forever remembered, forever sheltered, by your enduring, nurturing soul.

Love to you always,

M

Chapter 23

Memorandum to a Chambermaid...

"Looking back, though, I think it was no coincidence that I found myself in the television company of Mr. J.C. Watts, Jr., that evening. . . . God used the words of that speaker to reach out and straighten my uneven moral path."

Memorandum to a Chambermaid . . .

TO: Chambermaid, Marriott Hotel, St. Louis, Missouri
FROM: Martha Morgan Kern, Former Occupant of Room 1576
RE: A Mysterious Stack of Paper

While I certainly don't delude myself with the notion that you have been pacing the rooms of your life, trying to figure out why someone left an unexplained and out-of-place stack of paper in Room 1576 last summer, I felt it was important to write you. The story behind that paper means something to me; it marked a watershed moment in my experience, my full understanding, of ethics and honesty and upright behavior. If you don't mind, it will grant me a soothing sort of closure to tell you about it today.

We were in St. Louis on business, or at least my husband was. It was a routine, two-day trip for him, during which he would meet with customers and do whatever it is he does in his traveling mode. What was unusual about this particular trip was the presence of the rest of our family. My two sons and I don't customarily accompany my husband on his numerous professional junkets, but it was summer, the Cardinals were in town and playing right across the street from your hotel, and the grind of the school year loomed just ahead. So we packed our bags and went, taking up noisy and disheveled residence in two adjoining rooms, numbers 1576 and 1578, I believe, of the downtown Marriott.

In the grand scheme of things, it was a pleasant and fairly unremarkable stay. We had dinner and a paddle-boat ride at Union Station. We took in a Cardinals game (they lost to the Dodgers) on a clear, balmy night. The hotel swimming pool became one of our regular haunts, and it was en route to that very pool one day that the paper caper unfolded like an embarrassing and slightly surreal tabloid news item.

My husband was at a business appointment so it was just the boys and me, flip-flopping through the hotel corridors in our rubber-thonged pool shoes, carrying towels and books and maybe a set of goggles or two. The pool was in a different tower than our rooms were, so it was quite a trek. Our route led us past a labyrinth of paneled conference suites, all dark, empty, and weighted with the aura of impending decisions and slide-projector boredom. But one of them was lit, just recently abandoned by its suit-and-tie tenants, and on its long mahogany table lay neat rows of padded paper, emblazoned with the hotel logo, all left behind like yesterday's thoughts by those who had used or ignored them.

Now let me explain to you, Chambermaid, that as a writer and an inveterate maker of lists, I have an unnatural attraction to paper and pens; there is something especially tantalizing for me in the promising nib of an untried pen, in the reassuring heft of a tablet-full of paper. You could call it a fetish, but I prefer not to. Let's just say it's a fascination, a mild eccentricity, and leave it at that.

So there we were, alone in the inviting presence of at least twenty pads of paper, most missing just a few pages, and I was stopped in my tracks by the sheer wastefulness of that scene. What would become of all that paper? The hotel, to my thinking, would never present future business guests with recycled pads of paper, all vaguely scented with pastrami from someone else's lunch meeting, all lightly engraved with the impressions of a stranger's bold pen strokes. How second-rate that would seem! And in that short moment of odd reasoning, I made the choice to take those near-virgin pads for my own dull but essential purposes, possibly sparing them a trip to the hotel dumpster.

This theft was really a rescue mission, I told myself. I stationed my children as lookouts at the door; they were acutely uncomfortable with the whole scheme, in spite of my encouraging explanations, and they pleaded with me to hurry up or just forget this goofy idea. I should have listened. I should have thought about the terrible bind I put them in. But I didn't listen or think; instead I glided through the room, scooping up pad after pad like a vacuum sucking up dirt.

As is my custom when I've done something morally questionable, I tried to secure another person's approval; an ally always makes me feel better, as if their tacit endorsement will wipe the crime's oily coating from my soul. This time, it was my husband. I proudly showed him my paper haul, but to little avail. He was neither impressed nor visibly glad. He just shrugged and left me hanging there, unsure, guilty, alone in my contemplation of both the prize I had gained and the self-respect I had lost.

Later that night, I was laying on the bed, reading. The television was tuned to the Republican National Convention, and a gifted young speaker named J.C. Watts, Jr., was at the podium. I am not a fan of political conventions, Chambermaid, and I was tolerating its raucous noises only because my husband was engrossed in it. Looking back, though, I think it was no coincidence that I found myself in the television company of Mr. Watts that evening. I believe, in fact, that it was something of a miracle—God used the words of that speaker to reach out and straighten my uneven moral path.

As Mr. Watts was eloquently discussing ethics, a central topic in that election year, he said something like this: Ethical behavior is doing the right thing even when no one else is looking.

It is a simple idea, but an extremely meaningful one. It urges us to hold the same high moral standard at all times, even when illicit opportunities open up before us like tropical, fragrant blossoms. It speaks to the ethical compass embedded in each of us, the one that knows right from wrong and is unpersuaded by our elaborate rationales and polished excuses. I knew I had done the wrong thing in filching that paper; I could write poetry on each and every sheet, I could wrap gifts in its crisply textured folds, but I would never completely erase the ugly, gray smudges of my own ethical lapse.

So that is the reason you found that stack of paper in Room 1576 last summer. I couldn't remember which conference room it belonged in so I left it on our dresser in hopes that you would restore it to its rightful place. I'm sorry for that inconvenience, and I'm sorry I forgot, however temporarily, that doing the right thing is always more satisfying than choosing a darker alternative. Our secret sins are never really secret at all because we cannot hide them from ourselves. I have come to understand, Chambermaid, that even when it seems no one else is looking, someone always is.

Chapter 24

Dear Reader,

"Showing my feelings and wishes
and fears in the ink of this
page forces me to own them,
to take responsibility for them,
to do something about them."

Dear Reader,

Though we are strangers, you and I, I feel an attachment to you, a measure of gratitude, a slight stirring of connectedness that is almost certainly illusory. But it is there nonetheless, and I have come to rely on you. If you were not there to "hear" me, I would probably not bother to "speak." I don't need to see you; just imagining that you are there is enough to spur me on. Sometimes the passing of thoughts and feelings from one to another transcends identity, I think, and even occasionally celebrates its absence.

A long time ago, when I was about ten, my mother opened our front door to retrieve the paper and found a 45 record on our porch. On its sleeve was written: For Martha. There was no signature. Inside was The Herman's Hermits' hit, "There's a Kind of a Hush." It was, to my thinking, an anonymous declaration of love, the kind a girl can hold on to, reshape and reimagine, all the days of her life.

I never found out who left that record for me. It may have been my grandmother. It may have been the neighbor boy who clomped around in homemade shoes and used words like "specious." But I prefer to think that the record came from some shy boy I never noticed, a boy who one Saturday asked his mother to take him to the record shop downtown. He knew the record he wanted, and he paid for it with money saved from his allowance. In the early hours of that Sunday morning, he left the 45 on my doorstep, quietly, deftly, like a foot leaves an impression in the sand. He risked everything, then and there, and he risked nothing at all.

And so it is with me and the words on this page. I express myself to you, reader, like an old, trusted friend, someone with whom I can share my thoughts, my dark fears, my angst, my ecstasy. I stand behind the veil of this page and show you my soul in tiny increments. And you, with no name, no place in my daily life, listen quietly. I risk everything with you, and I risk nothing. You can pass me on the street and never connect me to my secrets. For me, it is a cozy, needed covenant.

Even now, as I write these thoughts, I am fooled by the intimacy of the moment. I am alone, writing on a legal pad. It is a safe place to be myself. I needn't wear a pleasant face or worry about the state of my hair. Small talk and pretense can be saved for another time. Into my mind I travel, bringing back surprising souvenirs to share with you, little fears and newfound truths

I have never before acknowledged, never confessed, never bothered to name and know like household pets. You may judge me, but I can't hear you. There is no freedom greater than this, Reader, none safer or more conducive to candor, exploration, the baring of my heart.

But when the work appears on the printed page the illusion of intimacy is washed away. I feel an electric sense of panic. My relatives may see this, my dentist, next-door neighbors, and casual acquaintances. People who know me will truly know me. Not the mother-and-wife me or the benign, social me who shops on Friday and chats on the phone. They will see the me that lives beneath my face and hordes petty secrets and private needs like a beggar hordes nickels. And if they judge me, I will hear them. There is no exposure starker than this, Reader, none scarier or less conducive to frank revelation and the baring of my heart.

My work has, on occasion, caused trouble in my life. I have said things on paper that people I know were not prepared to hear, much less to read in a book or magazine. Remembering their pain, I feel remorseful and self-conscious. While there is a huge part of me that wants to speak freely and truthfully, no matter the consequences, there is another that yearns for the warm caress of approval. I can think of nothing more dismal, more silencing, than exposing one's innermost thoughts and being rejected or ridiculed or dismissed as a liar. I am forever weighing the value of what feels like honest insight against my unceasing hunger for love and acceptance.

I could, of course, use a pseudonym and spare myself the agony of recognition. But I never have. There is a part of me that wants to be known. I don't want to pretend to be one thing when in my soul I feel I am another. There can be no greater waste of effort than the acting we do for one another, the subtle deceits we concoct to show that we are ever able, fearless, in control, and to conceal that we are not. We struggle to hide the fact that we struggle.

I can hide no more. I grew tired of it after a long life underground. It was a necessary part of growing up in a family where appearances counted more than what was real, and feelings were buried inside. There was violence at my house, and hard drinking. Dishes broke and bruises erupted in purple glory. My brother ran away and got in trouble with the police. It was a messy, messy life. But we never spoke of it, not with each other and certainly not with outsiders. We pretended to be normal, and it was an enormous effort; it required frequent lying and the making of many excuses. We probably did not fool everyone, but the people around us all played along and pretended not to know.

And to what end? I ask myself now. How were any of us helped by the masquerade? Perhaps my father's professional status would have slipped had our cover been blown. Friends might have shunned us, even if their own problems were just as consuming. But more than anything, we all feared exposure because it would force us to own our problems, to take responsibility for them and, ultimately, to *do* something about them. We would have had to change. We would have had to live in some other, alien way. The risk of something new and potentially difficult scared us even more than the tumultuous, sinking ship on which we stood.

If it is possible to be enslaved by the sameness of things, then I imagine it is possible to become hooked on self-examination and the change it often demands. I am thus addicted. Once I opened the box in which my interior life was locked, I could not shut it again. I look within it, Reader, and report to you its contents, over and over again.

And to what end? Why do I feel this need to communicate with you? I suppose I am simply mesmerized by the power of emotion and its heartfelt confession. It is worth the risk. Showing my feelings and wishes and fears in the ink of this page forces me to own them, to take responsibility for them, to do something about them. I want to be changed, affected, by the spirit within me.

These things I want, but not without a little safety. If I were always to say my thoughts aloud, I would risk too much. I cannot always trust myself to say things precisely as I mean them, and I cannot always trust myself to shut up when the time is right. But on this page, I am in control. I am not afraid, nor am I discouraged by the hurried look you might be wearing, or the discomfort that might collect around your eyes as I pour out my heart.

Here, I can put forth a perfected me, a grammatically-correct and multiply-rewritten version of myself that has been sanded smooth and framed like a picture. It's me, only better. It's me, though slightly more beguiling and ever more confident.

These words represent me in the same way that the words of a love song represented a boy from my childhood. He wanted his feelings known, but made slightly more beguiling and ever more romantic by a song, so that I might like them, so that I might like him. He left them on my doorstep, full of hope, a little tentative perhaps, just as I leave these words, my song, for you.

Gratefully,

M

Chapter 25

Dear God,

"It is time
to count my blessings,
to enumerate them one-by-one,
to take stock
of the world's beauty,
the rewards of
human existence, the intricacies
of life and my own place
within it."

Dear God,

I've been hearing quite a bit lately about the benefits of "journaling" and, more specifically, about a new permutation of that familiar idea—gratitude journaling. A popular author has published a gratitude journal to encourage mass participation, and Oprah Winfrey, a woman I respect immensely, is herself a devotee of this formal expression of thanks. I have decided, Father, that I too should try my hand at thankful thinking, examining and recording the bounty that is mine on a regular, prayerful basis.

It seems to me that focusing on what we have, no matter how small or commonplace, is a practice that far outshines our more innate tendency to obsess over what we have not. A change of perspective is in order. It is time to count my blessings, to enumerate them one-by-one, to take stock of the world's beauty, the rewards of human existence, the intricacies of life and my own place within it. It is time to make a habit of thanking you.

My journal is your journal—there can be no song of gratitude without the greater symphony of you. So it is to you that I address these thoughts, God, and it is to you that I owe this life of singular moments, this confluence of extraordinary details.

Today, I am grateful for these and many other things . . .

• The renewable quality of human life, the opportunities we all have to right what feels wrong and to reshape ourselves in the process.

• The smell of fresh-cut grass, and the way it hangs over summer neighborhoods like the bittersweet promise of rain.

• The warm, wriggly arrival of my sons beneath our quilt on Saturday morning, and the feeling that I'm needed in that drowsy tangle of arms and legs.

• The language of eyes and smiles and private expressions; the way my youngest son looks at me, with surreptitious love, when I come to help in his class at school.

• The reliable agreement of the seasons, as they graciously trade places, year after year, to bring majesty to our senses.

• The deep-pine aroma of Christmas, and the odd though marvelous tradition of bringing live, needly trees into the domesticated confines of houses.

• Candles burning in the dark; there is something sacred, hopeful, in those dancing lights.

• The lap-swish-rush rhythm of the ocean as it faithfully washes the shoreline.

• The million small choices in my past that ultimately formed the mosaic pattern of now.

• Fresh snow, and the softness it imposes on the world's sharp angles.

• My mother's macaroni and cheese.

• Old-fashioned, handwritten letters and the vibrant life stories they tell.

• Rich, black coffee, served in big, fat mugs.

• Long, interesting conversations that allow us to learn and be learned.

• The enlightening quality of a well-spun story.

• Spiritual gifts, their infinite diversity and boundless potential.

• Books, and the remarkable privilege of reading them.

• The invitation to escape, to fly over new territory, that is offered by an excellent movie.

• Wrigley Field, in spite of the Cubs.

• Cousins and aunts and uncles, parents and siblings and grandparents, all the kindred souls that are brought together by the inclusive net of family.

• The eloquent, timeless teachings of Jesus Christ.

• The freedom to choose my own paths, and the freedom to learn from each of them.

• The smell of bacon; it pulls me back through time to my mother's homey kitchen.

• The power and beauty of music.

• Life after thirty, and the sweet realization that "aging" is just another word for "growing."

Thank you, God, finally, for the carousel brilliance of the human condition.

Amen.

If you liked this book from ChariotVictor Publishing, check out this great title . . .

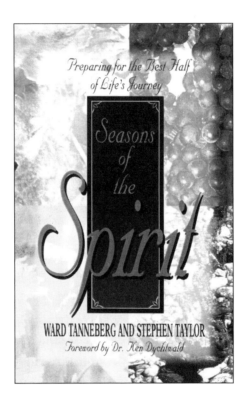

Combining allegory and practical application, the authors creatively help readers to reflect on the life that's past, examine their present situation and plan for a productive and fulfilling future. Using the cyclical patterns of a vineyard and the story of an "everyman" couple at midlife's crossroads, the authors make their points in a very engaging manner.

Seasons of the Spirit
by Ward Tanneberg, Ph.D.
and Stephen Taylor, Ph.D.
ISBN: 0-74593-852-3
Retail: $10.99 (U.S.)